CASE STUDIES
in Primary Care

A DAY IN
THE OFFICE

CASE STUDIES
in Primary Care

A DAY IN THE OFFICE

2nd Edition

Joyce D. Cappiello, PhD, FNP, FAANP
Assistant Professor of Nursing
University of New Hampshire
Durham, New Hampshire

Jeffrey A. Eaton, PhD, NP
Nurse Practitioner
Great Works Family Practice of York Hospital
South Berwick, Maine
Associate Professor
University of Southern Maine
Portland, Maine

Gene E. Harkless, DNSc, FNP-BC, CNL, FAANP
Chair
Associate Professor and Family Nurse Practitioner
Department of Nursing
University of New Hampshire
Durham, New Hampshire

ELSEVIER

ELSEVIER

3251 Riverport Lane
St. Louis, Missouri 63043

CASE STUDIES IN PRIMARY CARE: A DAY IN THE OFFICE,
SECOND EDITION

ISBN: 978-0-323-37812-3

Notices

Library of Congress Cataloging-in-Publication Data

Names: Eaton, Jeffrey A., author. | Cappiello, Joyce D., author. | Harkless,
  Gene E., author.
Title: Case studies in primary care : a day in the office / Joyce D.
  Cappiello, Jeffrey A. Eaton, Gene E. Harkless.
Other titles: Day in the office case studies in primary care
Description: 2nd edition. | St. Louis, Missouri : Elsevier, [2017] | Preceded
  by A day in the office case studies in primary care / Jeffrey A. Eaton,
  Joyce D. Cappiello. c1998. | Includes index.
Identifiers: LCCN 2016019786 | ISBN 9780323378123
Subjects: | MESH: Primary Health Care--methods | Medical History
  Taking--methods | Diagnosis, Differential | Patient Care Planning | Case
  Reports
Classification: LCC RC66 | NLM W 84.6 | DDC 362.1--dc23 LC record available at https://lccn.loc.gov/2016019786

Content Strategist: Lee Henderson
Content Development Manager: Billie Sharp
Publishing Services Manager: Hemamalini Rajendrababu
Project Manager: Maria Luisa Ordonio
Design Direction: Renee Duenow

Printed in China

Last digit is the print number: 9 8 7 6 5 4 3 2

Acknowledgments

Thanks to the willingness of so many of our colleagues to contribute to this book. Also thank you to the faculty and students (past and present) of the Department of Nursing at UNH and the School of Nursing at USM for their collegiality, and direct and indirect contributions to this book.

We would also like to recognize Charlotte Paolini and the late Howard Barrows for opening us up to the world of Problem-Based Learning.

Thanks to my husband, Dan, for his patience with the revision of this book and to all of my family: Nick, Maggie, Charlie, Caroline, Lena, Brent, Bella, Gracie, Anna, and Ben. You have enriched my life more than I can ever express.

Joyce D. Cappiello

Special thanks to my family: my wife Janet, my children Carla, Colin (and Amanda), and Cody … and to my grandson Jonah, who makes being a grandfather all they say it is.

Jeffrey A. Eaton

And, along with Jeff and Joyce, I want to thank my incredibly patient husband, Peter Farrell, along with my daughters, Anne, Jane, and Megan Farrell, for their steadfast encouragement and love. And for those many who have created the path forward for us, we are forever grateful.

Gene E. Harkless

Contributors
and Reviewers

Contributors

Nancy G. Baugh, PhD, MSN, BSN, ANP
Associate Professor/Director
Franklin Pierce University
Portsmouth, New Hampshire

Wendy I. Biddle, PhD, MSN, RN, FNP-BC
Program Director, MSN-FNP
College of Nursing and Public Health
South University
Nurse Practitioner
Gastroenterology LTD
Virginia Beach, Virginia

Maureen Boardman, BSN, MSN
Clinical Assistant Professor of Medicine
Geisel School of Medicine at Dartmouth
Hanover, New Hampshire
Director of Clinical Quality
Little Rivers Health Care
Bradford, Vermont

**Nancy E. Dirubbo, DNP, FNP-BC, FAANP,
Certificate In Travel Health**
President
Travel Health of New Hampshire
Laconia, New Hampshire

Adele Susan Feeney, DNP, APRN, FNP-BC, NP-C
Assistant Professor, Family Nurse Practitioner
   Program Coordinator
Graduate School of Nursing
University of Massachusetts Worcester
Worcester, Massachusetts
Senior Faculty
Fitzgerald Health Education Associates, Inc.
North Andover, Massachusetts

Chrissie Ferreri, DNP, APRN, FNP-BC
Nurse Practitioner
Elliot Pediatrics
New Hampshire Hospital for Children
Manchester, New Hampshire
Adjunctive Faculty
Graduate School of Nursing
University of New Hampshire
Durham, New Hampshire

Loren Fields, MSN
Lecturer
Midwifery and Women's Health
Yale School of Nursing
Nurse Practitioner
Planned Parenthood of Southern New England
New Haven, Connecticut

Sarah Hallen, MD
Assistant Professor
Internal Medicine/Geriatric Medicine
Tufts University School of Medicine
Boston, Massachusetts
Fellowship Director
Geriatric Medicine
Maine Medical Center
Portland, Maine

Gail Handwork, APRN, DCNP
Dermatology
Foundation Skin Surgery and Dermatology
Nashua, New Hampshire
President
New England Dermatology Nurse Practitioners
    Association
Burlington, Massachusetts

Donna Lawlor, DNP, ANP-C
Assistant Professor
University of Southern Maine
Portland, Maine

Patricia Thompson Leavitt, DNP, FNP
Assistant Professor
Nursing
University of Southern Maine
Portland, Maine
Executive Director
Leavitt's Mill Free Health Center
Buxton, Maine

Amy Levi, PhD, CNM, WHNP-BC
Leah L. Albers Professor of Midwifery
College of Nursing
University of New Mexico
Albuquerque, New Mexico

Michele Loos, MS, APRN, FNP-C
Clinical Assistant Professor
Nursing
University of New Hampshire
Durham, New Hampshire
Nurse Practitioner
Supportive and Palliative Care
Wentworth-Douglass Hospital
Nurse Practitioner
Prompt Care
Wentworth Health Partners
Dover, New Hampshire

Colleen Sullivan Lynch, RN, MS, FNP-C
Adjunct Faculty
Nursing
University of New Hampshire
Durham, New Hampshire
Family Nurse Practitioner
Wentworth-Douglass Hospital
Dover, New Hampshire

Kerry Nolte, PhD, FNP-C
Clinical Assistant Professor
Nursing
University of New Hampshire
Durham, New Hampshire
Nursing
Northeastern University
Boston, Massachusetts

Donna Pelletier, DNP, MS, BS
Clinical Associate Professor
Nursing
University of New Hampshire
Durham, New Hampshire

Cheri Sarton, PhD, CNM
Assistant Professor
Nursing
University of Southern Maine
Portland, Maine

Evie Stacy, MS, APRN
Pediatric Nurse Practitioner
Neurology Department
Dartmouth Hitchcock Clinic
Manchester, New Hampshire
Medical Director
Spaulding Youth Center
Northfield, New Hampshire

Annelle Taylor, BA, MSN
Nurse Practitioner
Women's Health and Adult Primary Care
The South Bronx Health Center/Montefiore
    Medical Center
Bronx, New York

Reviewers

**Sameeya Ahmed-Winston, MSN, CPNP,
    CPHON, BMTCN**
Pediatric Nurse Practitioner
Blood and Marrow Transplant Unit
Children's National Medical Center
Washington, DC

**Margaret-Ann Carno, PhD, RN, MBA, MJ,
    CPNP, D, ABSM, FAAN**
Professor of Clinical Nursing and Pediatrics
University of Rochester, School of Nursing
Rochester, New York

**Kathleen Sanders Jordan, DNP, MS, RN,
    FNP-BC, ENP-BC, SANE-P**
Clinical Assistant Professor
Graduate School of Nursing
The University of North Carolina Charlotte
    Graduate School of Nursing
Nurse Practitioner
Emergency Department
Mid-Atlantic Emergency Medicine Associates
Charlotte, North Carolina

**Vanessa M. Kalis DNP, APRN, CNS, RN,
    PNP-AC, ACNP-BC**
Director, Acute Care DNP Programs
Musco School of Nursing and Health Professions
Brandman University
Irvine, California

Pamela L. King, PhD, FNP, PNP, FAANP, APRN
Nursing
Spalding University
Louisville, Kentucky

Laura Steadman EdD, MSN, CRNP
Assistant Professor
Adult, Acute Health, Chronic Care and
    Foundations
The University of Alabama at Birmingham
Birmingham, Alabama

Robin Webb Corbett, PhD, RN-C, FNP-BC
Associate Professor
Nursing Graduate
Interim–Chair Graduate Nursing Science
East Carolina University
Greenville, North Carolina

Introduction

To the Instructor

Case Studies in Primary Care: A Day in the Office was written to provide primary care instructors and students with "real-world" scenarios from which to teach and learn the clinical reasoning skills needed in today's primary care settings. The second edition of this popular workbook will help to address the growing need among master's-level Nurse Practitioner (NP) programs, doctoral-level NP programs including Doctor of Nursing Practice (DNP) programs, and Physician Assistant (PA) programs, with authentic, high-quality case studies for problem-based learning.

Like the popular first edition, the second edition portrays the real world of primary care in the context of two realistic clinical days, and teaches students to carefully analyze various clinical situations in order to deliver high-quality care. It has been written with the objective of allowing a student or clinician to go through the clinical reasoning process just as it would occur in an office setting. All of the cases are realistic because the book is based on actual patients, or composites of patients, who have been cared for by the clinicians contributing to this book. Actual cases are used because actual cases represent "ill-structured" problems like those encountered in office practice. "Textbook cases" occur primarily in textbooks, and not in clinical practice. Identifying information has, of course, been changed to protect privacy. In the cases where composites have been used, this has been done to protect individual privacy rather than to create a case reflecting a specific pathology. In cases where a composite has been used, several clinicians have reviewed the case to ensure that it is a plausible scenario.

The second edition includes 50 case studies on many of the most commonly encountered clinical situations seen in primary care settings. Six of the cases are entirely new, and all of the cases are thoroughly revised to reflect the latest research evidence and clinical practice guidelines. The cases cover all age groups seen in family practice, as well as reflecting a contemporary appreciation of gender and cultural diversity. Selected cases have been refocused to reflect current practice environments, including follow-up care of patients coming to the primary care setting from retail clinics, rehabilitation settings, or acute-care settings.

The cases have been reviewed by experienced NPs, PAs, and physicians. Although every reasonable effort has been made to ensure that the information presented is correct, it must of course be accepted that healthcare is a rapidly changing discipline, and that new knowledge may be available that was not accessible when this book was written. Because the ultimate decision and responsibility for patient care belongs to the individual clinician, cases in which you or a student disagrees with what is written may actually provide a greater opportunity for discussion and learning. This book is not intended to be a textbook, but rather an opportunity to develop and exercise one's knowledge and abilities.

Each of the cases begins with an Opening Scenario, which varies in detail from case to case, just as a practitioner would find in a typical primary care setting. An attempt has been made to organize each case into the following consistent sections:

- History of Present Illness
- Medical History
- Family Medical History
- Social History
- Medications
- Allergies
- Review of Systems
- Physical Examination

Although the structure of each case is consistent (except for those focused on telephone calls, lab follow-ups, or alternative scenarios), the cases are subtly different in emphasis. This is a deliberate effort to stimulate different portions of the clinical reasoning process. In some cases, readers will be asked to make decisions with limited information, and in others they will be given far more information than would actually be available in a clinical encounter. In each case, the objective is for the reader to ask: "Do I need this information?" "How can I use this information?" "What does this information really mean?"

After analyzing the cases, students are asked to identify and write down any "Learning Issues" specific to the case, which call for them to begin a "learning practice" based on the most recent scientific evidence. Students are then asked to develop an Assessment and Plan and write them in the printed workbook. Once students are satisfied with their handwritten plans, they are asked to type their answers into the book's online answer submission tool at http://evolve.elsevier.com/Cappiello for grading. To guide students in developing their Learning Issues, Assessment, and Plan, a Grading Criteria rubric is provided as an appendix and on the Evolve site.

After students have clicked the "Submit" button to submit their answers for grading, the students' answers are sent to you for grading via an email address that you will have entered within the "asset settings" on the Evolve website. To learn how to set up the Evolve website for this grading functionality, please go to http://evolve.elsevier.com/Cappiello and navigate to Instructor Resources/How to Set Up the Online Case Study Submission. To assist you in grading, an instructor-oriented Grading Rubric is also provided in the Evolve Instructor Resources.

Once the student's answers to a case are submitted, they will have immediate access to the Feedback for that particular case. (This Feedback is available to instructors at any time via Evolve access provided by your Elsevier representative for as long as you continue to require student purchase of the book.) If the student does not get the opportunity to review the Feedback immediately upon submission, the feedback will only become available once it is "unlocked" by the instructor. The Feedback illustrates expert clinical judgment processes for students to compare against their own clinical reasoning. The Feedback for each case is organized into the following sections, although there may be exceptions where other pertinent sections are included:

- Learning Issues
- Initial Ideas
- Interpretation of Cues, Patterns, and Information
- Revised Ideas
- Diagnostic Options
- Therapeutic Options
- Follow-up
- References

References are provided for two reasons. The first is to provide documentation of the accuracy of information. The second is to offer an opportunity for additional investigation of a particular topic area. References may include recent reputable websites, textbooks, e-textbooks, pocket references, or mobile apps that are used by clinicians in day-to-day practice. In some cases, a current article is cited to provide emerging information or because it provides a succinct overview. Key websites, such as that of the Centers for Disease Control and Prevention (CDC), have a wealth of current information directed to the healthcare provider. The references are a mix of primary references and research with practical, easy-to-use references for a busy clinician. We practice in a changing world, and the number of internet-based references has grown substantially since the publication of the first edition. Critically evaluating and choosing online resources will be an important skill for clinicians of this generation. It is hoped that it will become apparent to the reader when additional references are necessary, or when they would enhance clinical practice.

This book is intended to allow students and beginning clinicians to exercise their clinical reasoning abilities to the extent possible in this format. Our students' feedback has been that the cases are extremely helpful for clinical learning. In fact, these students have often contributed great insights that have strengthened these cases. We hope that others will also find them useful.

Joyce D. Cappiello PhD, FNP, FAANP
Jeffrey A. Eaton PhD, NP
Gene E. Harkless, DNSc, FNP-BC, CNL, FAANP

To the Student

Case Studies in Primary Care: A Day in the Office was written to provide you with "real-world" scenarios from which to learn the clinical reasoning skills needed in today's primary care settings. The book portrays the real world of primary care in the context of two realistic clinical days, and demonstrates how to carefully analyze various clinical situations in order to deliver high-quality care. It has been written with the objective of allowing you to go through the clinical reasoning process just as you would in an office setting.

All of the cases are realistic because the book is based on actual patients, or composites of patients, who have been cared for by the clinicians contributing to the book. Identifying information has, of course, been changed to protect privacy. Actual cases are used because actual cases represent "ill-structured" problems like those encountered in office practice. "Textbook cases" occur primarily in textbooks and not in clinical practice.

The second edition includes 50 case studies on many of the most commonly encountered clinical situations seen in primary care settings. The cases cover all age groups seen in family practice, as well as reflecting a contemporary appreciation of gender and cultural diversity. Selected cases include follow-up care of patients coming to the primary care setting from retail clinics, rehabilitation settings, or acute-care settings, to reflect current practice environments.

The cases have been reviewed by experienced NPs, PAs, and physicians. Although every reasonable effort has been made to ensure that the information presented is correct, it must of course be accepted that healthcare is a rapidly changing discipline, and that new knowledge may be available that was not accessible when this book was written. Because the ultimate decision and responsibility for patient care belongs to the individual clinician, cases in which you disagree with what is written may actually provide a greater opportunity for discussion and learning. This book is not intended to be a textbook, but rather an opportunity to develop and exercise your knowledge and abilities.

Each of the cases begins with an Opening Scenario, which varies in detail from case to case, just as a practitioner would find in a typical primary care setting. An attempt has been made to organize each case into the following consistent sections:

- History of Present Illness
- Medical History
- Family Medical History
- Social History
- Medications
- Allergies
- Review of Systems
- Physical Examination

Although the structure of each case is generally consistent, the cases are subtly different. This is a deliberate effort to stimulate different portions of the clinical reasoning process. In some cases, you will be asked to make decisions with limited information, and in others you will be given far more information than would actually be available in a clinical encounter. In each case the objective is for you to ask: "Do I need this information?" "How can I use this information?" "What does this information really mean?"

After analyzing the cases, you are asked to identify and write down any "Learning Issues" specific to the case, which call for you to begin a "learning practice" based on the most recent scientific evidence. You are then asked to develop an Assessment and Plan and write them in the printed workbook. Once you are satisfied with your hand-written plans, you are then asked to type your answers into the book's online answer submission tool at http://evolve.elsevier.com/Cappiello for grading. To guide you in developing your Learning Issues, Assessment, and Plan, a Grading Criteria rubric is provided as an appendix, as well as on the Evolve site.

As you consider each case, you will want to keep in mind the following factors:

Schedule. Consider the time of day and length of visit for which each patient is scheduled. Time restraints should be considered, and appropriate strategies thought through, such as using a follow-up visit for further evaluation or intervention.

Learning Issues. Healthcare is a learning profession. As you encounter each patient, you will often need to gather new or updated evidence for practice. Thus, you will need to consider Learning Issues for each case before completing the Assessment and Plan sections. Students often have a difficult time deciding how to approach a problem, especially early in their education. By contrast, experienced clinicians may focus in on one diagnosis or option, without consciously considering all possibilities. In many cases this is not a defect in the clinical reasoning of the experienced clinician, but a way to expedite the clinical reasoning process. When an experienced clinician encounters an unfamiliar or otherwise "ill-structured" problem, however, the ability to think things through deliberately and systematically becomes important. Some references refer to this increased attention to the process of how we are thinking through problems as being "metacognitive."

Questions to Consider. If you find yourself perplexed on where to begin thinking through a patient's problems, the following questions may help you begin this thought process:

- *Even before I go in the room, what do I think is going on?*
- *Is this person's age important?*
- *Are biological sex or gender roles important to this case?*
- *What are common causes of this problem in this geographical area or population?*
- *What is my objective for this visit? Is it just to address the identified problem or to do a more general assessment?*
- *What do I need to know about this complaint?*
- *How will I organize my data collection?*
- *How should I relate to the patient and/or family?*
- *What other past medical history do I need?*
- *What social history do I need?*
- *Do I need to assess for substance misuse?*
- *Do I need family history?*
- *What kind of a review of systems should I perform?*
- *Have I asked about medication and allergy history?*

- *Have I asked about over-the-counter and herbal medications?*
- *What data, including physical examination, laboratory test, and/or imaging studies, will help me confirm or refute my diagnostic hypothesis?*
- *Do I know how to perform the physical examination techniques needed to assess this complaint?*
- *Have I considered the sensitivity, specificity, and likelihood ratio in deciding what physical examination component or test to use?*
- *What is on my differential diagnosis list? (Have I included both the things that are probable and the things that are potentially serious?)*
- *Do I need a consultation?*
- *If I decide to treat, what are my treatment options?*
- *Is cost a factor in choosing a treatment?*
- *Have I negotiated a treatment plan with the patient and/or family so that it is congruent with their expectations and abilities?*
- *Are there health maintenance or health promotion needs for this patient? Should I address these on this visit, or is a follow-up visit necessary?*
- *Does this patient need follow-up for the presenting complaint?*
- *How will I know if the treatment has been effective?*
- *What cultural factors may be important in the diagnosis or treatment of this problem?*
- *Is there anything else I should be thinking about?*

For reference, you will find these questions reproduced inside the book's back cover.

Each clinician will find a way of organizing the collection, evaluation, and synthesis of information that fits that individual's style. As you consider these cases, however, you may wish to approach them using the same structure in which Expert Feedback will be presented to you after online submission of your answers:

- Initial Ideas
- Interpretation of Cues, Patterns, and Information
- Revised Ideas
- Diagnostic Options
- Therapeutic Options
- Follow-up

After carefully considering a case, note your preliminary thoughts or answers by writing in the answer spaces provided in the printed book. When you are ready to submit your responses for the Learning Issues, Assessment, and Plan for instructor grading and expert feedback on the case, go to http://www.evolve.elsevier.com/Cappiello/ as directed by your instructor. You will receive the Feedback immediately after you have clicked the "Submit" button for a particular case. For grading, the answers are sent to your instructor via email. If you do not get the opportunity to review the Feedback immediately upon submission, the Feedback will only become available once it is "unlocked" by your instructor. The Feedback illustrates expert clinical judgment processes for you to compare against your own clinical reasoning. The Feedback for each case is organized into the following sections, although there may be exceptions where other pertinent sections are included:

- Learning Issues
- Initial Ideas
- Interpretation of Cues, Patterns, and Information
- Revised Ideas
- Diagnostic Options
- Therapeutic Options
- Follow-up
- References and Further Readings

This Feedback is intended to provide a basis for comparison to other clinicians' learning needs and approaches, and is not intended to be interpreted as "right" answers. In fact, there is no single right answer in the vast majority of cases you will encounter, but the range of options will be defined by a rational, evidence-based approach to clinical problems. Unfortunately, there is not always research evidence available, or research may be flawed or contradictory. Feedback is provided to show opinions from the literature, as well as other anecdotal information when appropriate. The Feedback reflects the synthesis of current information by experienced clinicians. We believe the Feedback to be, in all cases, a reasonable approach to the problem described. It may not, however, be the best approach for another given patient or a given clinician, or additional knowledge may exist in the future that would change the possible outcome of the case. In primary care, the right answer may depend on the resources of the client and practitioner, and may vary greatly from instance to instance. You may create a more complete or elegant approach than that described in the Feedback.

Learning Issues. The Learning Issues Feedback provides issues that have been generated by the authors and previous tutorial groups. This section is not meant to be exhaustive, and you will often have very different Learning Issues, depending on your own levels of development.

Initial Ideas. When a clinician sees a problem on the schedule of patients, or hears an initial complaint, ideas are quickly generated as to the etiology of the problem and its possible treatments. Rather than deny that this process exists, it is worthwhile to acknowledge and utilize it to achieve positive results while preventing or minimizing any negative results. Further, these initial ideas will drive the collection of data.

Interpretation of Cues, Patterns, and Information. Symptom analysis is the process by which most clinicians begin collecting data. One mnemonic that may help in the collection of data is OPQRST:

O: Are Other people sick?
P (2): Provocative and Palliative actions. What makes it better? What makes it worse?
Q (2): Quality and Quantity of the pain?
R (3): Region, Radiation, Recurrence. Where is it? Does it go anywhere else? Have you ever had this before?

S (2): <u>S</u>everity, <u>S</u>ymptoms. Similar to quantity but may have a somewhat more subjective flavor. Do you have any other symptoms?

T (3): <u>T</u>iming, <u>T</u>emporality, <u>T</u>reatment. When did it first come on? What time of day is it better or worse? What other treatments have you tried?

Although OPQRST does not necessarily allow for a story to be told, in its most logical form it is a valuable mechanism to review a patient story, to ensure that the necessary information has been obtained. OLDCARTS (<u>O</u>nset, <u>L</u>ocation/radiation, <u>D</u>uration, <u>C</u>haracter, <u>A</u>ggravating factors, <u>R</u>elieving factors, <u>T</u>iming, and <u>S</u>everity) is another often-used alternative.

Once data are collected, certain patterns may appear that support or dispute a particular etiology for the patient's problem. These patterns are interpreted based on the knowledge base and the experience of the clinician. These patterns may indicate the need for further investigation through history, physical examination, or other diagnostic testing, or they may lead to a specific theory of the cause of the problem or problems.

Revised Ideas. Once appropriate history and physical examination have been completed, there will be new thoughts about the most probable causes of the patient problem. The emerging differential diagnoses will drive much of your data collection. A differential diagnosis is merely a "laundry list" of the possible causes for a particular symptom, sign, or syndrome. Most clinicians include four to six possibilities in their working differential. Usually these possibilities are the most common and/or the most dangerous causes of the signs or symptoms. The differential diagnosis is an excellent guide to action because the objective is to rule in, or rule out, the possibilities. A symptom may have more than one cause, so it may be necessary to rule out problems on the differential even when another possibility has been ruled in. For example, even when history findings are conclusive that a viral illness is present, in a patient with pharyngitis it may be necessary to test for Strep infection to eliminate the possibility of coexisting viral and bacterial infections.

A word about "zebras." There is an old adage in clinical practice: "When you hear hoofbeats, look for horses before you look for zebras." Though there is great truth to this adage, one cannot forget that occasionally a zebra (a rare or dangerous condition) will occur. Patients ask their healthcare providers to provide them with the greatest assurance possible that they do not have a dangerous condition. Often just a few strategic history questions or physical assessment techniques can rule out potentially dangerous conditions. Laboratory and other diagnostic tests must be used judiciously.

Diagnostic Options. Many times after a patient encounter is completed, the clinician has a working diagnosis but does not necessarily have a definite answer of what is wrong. Trials of therapy, laboratory work, or other diagnostic testing, or referral to another provider, are all options. All treatment options must be based on efficacy and safety.

Therapeutic Options. The role of the clinician is to inform and facilitate patient decision making. Often you are presenting several choices to the patient. For example,

"We could begin with medication or physical therapy. Here are the advantages and disadvantages of each approach." There may be barriers of cost, transportation to the pharmacy or physical therapy, difficulty of swallowing pills, or other issues that need sorting out. Are there educational needs of the patient and/or the family? Are there specific cultural issues to address? This book approaches provider-patient communication using the principles of shared decision making as a means of consideration of patient preferences, values, and context.

Pharmacological. When choosing a medication, there are many different factors to consider. What is the drug of choice for this problem? Are there other factors to consider (allergies, pregnancy, or drug interactions)? What is the best route and dosage for this patient?

Nonpharmacological. Included in this section are options such as physical therapy, culturally prescribed approaches, and alternative therapies.

Educational. When caring for an individual, there must be recognition that the individual and/or family are really the ones who determine what treatment will be carried out. Patient-centered education is essential.

Social Determinants of Health. We recognize that many factors beyond the door of the clinic affect health outcomes. Racism and subsequent health disparities affect health and wellness for many of the patients that we see. It is our hope that the social determinants of health are explored, such as, "What if this patient lived in poverty? What if this patient lived in a rural area versus an urban area? What if this patient is African American, Hispanic, or another minority? What if this patient has an illegal immigrant status?" You also need to consider whether the patient's sexuality and gender identity may affect care. Lesbian, gay, bisexual, transgender, or queer (LGBTQ) patients may have different needs, and awareness of this issue can help prevent inappropriate care recommendations. The list of factors is potentially long; however, the underlying principle of applying the concepts of the social determinants of health to patients seen in your specific clinic or geographical area should provide the foundation of your care.

Follow-up. It is often a challenge for a fledgling clinician to decide when (and if) to ask a patient to return for a follow-up visit. Should the patient return if there is no improvement, or should a recheck be scheduled whether the patient feels that he or she has improved or not? Is phone follow-up appropriate? Research in this area is limited, so the individual clinician must often wrestle with this issue.

References. References are provided in the Feedback for two reasons. The first is to provide documentation of the accuracy of information. The second is to offer an opportunity for additional investigation of a particular topic area. References may include recent reputable websites, textbooks, e-textbooks, pocket references, or mobile apps that are used by clinicians in day-to-day practice. In some cases a current article is cited to provide emerging information or because it provides a succinct overview. Key websites, such as that of the Centers for Disease Control and Prevention (CDC), have a wealth of current information directed to the healthcare provider. The references are a mix of primary references and research with practical, easy-to-use references for a busy clinician. We practice in a changing world, and the number of internet-based references has grown substantially since the publication of the first edition. Critically evaluating and choosing online resources will be an important skill for clinicians of this generation. It is hoped that it will become apparent to the reader when additional references are necessary, or when they would enhance clinical practice.

This book is intended to allow students and beginning clinicians to exercise their clinical reasoning abilities to the extent possible in this format. Our students' feedback has been that the cases are extremely helpful for clinical learning. In fact, these students have often contributed great insights that have strengthened these cases. We hope that others will also find them useful.

Joyce D. Cappiello PhD, FNP, FAANP
Jeffrey A. Eaton PhD, NP
Gene E. Harkless DNSc, FNP-BC, CNL, FAANP

Contents

Day One

Day Two

DAY ONE

Case 1

Organizing and Managing Your Day

· ·

You are starting at a new practice. The office manager introduces you to the staff and then asks you, "How do you like to work? Are there any questions you have that we can answer that could make your work and life life easier?"

How will you respond to the office manager's query?

Jot down your notes or preliminary answers in the space provided below. When you are ready to submit your answers for grading (if you are working with an instructor) and reflective feedback to help you evaluate your answers, go to **http://www.evolve.elsevier.com/Cappiello/** to complete this case.

Learning Issues

Identify any learning issues that you believe are important for you to explore about this case. (This case will not require an Assessment and Plan per se.)

Case 2

Harold Baron

Age 56 years

Opening Scenario

Harold Baron is a 56-year-old African American man on your schedule for an annual health-care visit. He wants to start an exercise program. He has been seen in your practice for the past three years for episodic visits but has never been seen for health maintenance.

History of Present Illness

"I feel that I'm getting older and I've put on a few pounds, so I think I should start exercising. I'll probably just start out with brisk walking, but I'd like to get up to running a few miles a day. I feel very healthy."

Medical History

Denies chronic illness: No history of heart disease, HTN, or diabetes. Tonsillectomy and adenoidectomy as a child. Denies previous colonoscopy (screening or diagnostic)

Immunizations: Reports usual childhood immunizations; denies hepatitis A or B immunization; unsure of last tetanus immunization Has never received seasonal influenza immunization.

Last laboratory tests more than five years ago, per patient; unsure what was tested but were "all normal."

Family Medical History

MGM: Died at age 82 (breast cancer)
MGF: Died at age 77 (myocardial infarction)
PGM: Died at age 80 (complications of type 2 DM)
PGF: Died at age 74 (stroke)
Mother: 81 years old (type 2 DM)
Father: Died at age 80 (stroke two years ago)
Brother: 58 years old (type 2 DM)

Daughter: 32 years old (A&W)
Son: 30 years old (A&W)
Four grandchildren: None with health problems

Social History

Married for 34 years; works full time as administrator in a post office, extensive com-
   puter use; no recreational exercise; quit smoking 15 years ago (25 pack-year history)
Alcohol: Three ounces per week (glass of wine)
Caffeine: Two cups of coffee per day
Safety: Wears seatbelt; does ride bicycle in summer on occasion and wears helmet;
   does not ride motorcycles; does not wear sunscreen

Medications

One multivitamin "for men" daily, last dose this AM
Vitamin D 1000 IU daily, last dose this AM
Acetaminophen 325 mg, two tablets once or twice daily for one to three days per week
   for knee pain, last dose two days ago

Allergies

NKDA

Review of Systems

General: Good energy level, denies fatigue; sleeps approximately seven hours a night;
   denies snoring, difficulty initiating or maintaining sleep; wakes rested and denies
   daytime drowsiness
Integumentary: Denies new lesions, itching, or rashes
HEENT: Denies history of head injury; denies eye pain, excessive tearing, blurring, or
   change in vision; denies tinnitus or vertigo; denies frequent colds, seasonal allergies,
   or sinus problems; dental examination with cleaning every six months; wears nonpre-
   scription glasses for reading only; eye examination (without dilation) 12 months ago
Neck: Denies lumps, swollen glands, goiter, or pain
Cardiovascular: Denies chest pain, shortness of breath, or elevated blood pressure;
   denies swelling in extremities. Denies excessive bruising, enlarged lymph glands;
   denies history of transfusions
Respiratory: Denies shortness of breath, cough, dyspnea, wheeze, orthopnea, snoring
Gastrointestinal: Denies nausea or vomiting, constipation, or diarrhea; denies heartburn, belching, bloating, stomach pain, black or clay-colored stools; denies having
   had a colonoscopy

Genitourinary: Denies dysuria, frequency, urgency, difficulty starting or stopping stream, and any sexual dysfunction; libido normal

Musculoskeletal: Right knee pain (4 out of 10) described as achy noted with prolonged walking, standing, climbing stairs; gradual onset present intermittently for past year; denies trauma to knee; denies swelling, redness, warmth; denies any other joint pain/ache; denies back pain

Neurological: Occasional (fewer than once per week) mild headache (bilateral frontal pressure) relieved by acetaminophen 325 mg; denies severe headaches; denies numbness/tingling, weakness; denies history of seizures, head trauma

Endocrine: No polyuria, polyphagia, polydipsia; denies history of thyroid disorder

Physical Examination

Vital signs: Temperature 98.4° F; pulse 74/bpm; respiration 20/min; BP 132/80 mm Hg

Height: 5 ft 9 in; *weight:* 178 lb; *BMI:* 26.3

General: Well nourished, well developed; in no acute distress; appears younger than stated age

HEENT: Normocephalic without masses or lesions; pupils equal, round, and reactive to light; extraocular movements intact; fundi with crisp disc margins, no evidence of retinopathy; nares patent and noninjected; pharynx without redness or lesions

Skin: No atypical lesions, rashes, visible scars; nails normal without lines or pitting; head shaved with appearance of male pattern baldness noted

Neck: Supple without thyromegaly, adenopathy, or carotid bruits

Heart: Regular rate and rhythm; no murmurs, rubs; no S3, no S4; PMI at left 5th ICS, MCL

Lungs: Clear to auscultation

Abdomen: No hepatosplenomegaly; soft, nontender; bowel sounds normoactive; abdominal aorta, renal, and iliac arteries without bruits

Genitourinary: Normal male; circumcised; both testicles descended, smooth without nodules or abnormalities; no inguinal bulge discernable

Rectal: Prostate slightly enlarged symmetrically, obliterated median sulcus, smooth, firm

Musculoskeletal: Spine full range of motion; bilateral extremities: full range of motion without pain or limitation; bilateral knees: no ballottement, negative bulge sign, negative drawer, Lachman's, and McMurray's tests

Neuromuscular: Normal stance and gait; reflexes 2+ at Achilles, patellar, biceps, triceps, and brachioradialis

Peripheral vascular: No cyanosis, clubbing, or edema; femoral, popliteal, pedal pulses +2 equal bilaterally; no varicosities

Lymph: Head/neck, groin, axillae without adenopathy

After reviewing the case and the Grading Criteria in Appendix A, jot down your notes or preliminary answers in the spaces provided below. When you are ready to submit your answers for grading (if you are working with an instructor) and reflective feedback to help you evaluate your answers, go to **http://www.evolve.elsevier.com/Cappiello/** to complete this case.

Learning Issues

Before identifying your recommended Assessment and Plan, identify any learning issues that you believe are important for you to explore about this case:

Assessment

Please indicate the problems or issues you have identified that will guide your care (preferably in list form):

Continued

Plan

Please list your plans for addressing each of the problems or issues in your assessment:

Case 3

Polly Latour
Age 81 years

Opening Scenario

Polly Latour is an 81-year-old woman on your schedule for incontinence that she has had for many years. Her usual provider will be out on maternity leave for at least the next three months. This is her first visit to your practice.

History of Present Illness

Mrs. Latour relates that she has been having problems over the past 15 years with "losing her urine." She notes that this has happened for no apparent reason. All of a sudden she feels like she has to go and, by the time she gets to the bathroom, usually her pad or "adult diaper" is wet. She voids in fairly large amounts. She has no dysuria and no difficulty starting stream. Occasionally she also loses her urine when she coughs and, at times, when she is lifting or carrying things. She has a known history of two to three UTIs per year. Menopause occurred at age 44 (surgical). She tries to void every hour to minimize incontinence.

Medical History

TIA about 15 years ago—word finding, right leg tingling, lasted about 30 minutes; no symptoms since
HTN, hyperlipidemia
Breast biopsy at age 55
Cataract surgeries with lens implants × 2, five and seven years ago
DJD in both hips (left side worse than right side)
Hysterectomy with BSO at age 44 for menometrorrhagia

Family Medical History

Mother: Deceased at age 68 (DM [onset at age 66], had a fall and got "bleeding in her brain")
Father: Deceased at age 69 (lung cancer from smoking; bladder cancer)

Sister: 78 years old, retired nurse (mild DM)
Daughter: 58 years old (mild HTN)

Social History

Lives with her wife Lucille. They have been together for the past 30 years, although they married just last year. Ex-husband died 10 years ago; they had a cordial relationship. One pack per day (ppd) smoker until age 30. Has not smoked since. One alcoholic drink per year. Did some retail work but mostly at home. Daughter (58 years old) is an investment advisor and lives about 1000 miles away. Daughter is divorced and has two daughters of her own, ages 35 and 33. No great-grandchildren.

Medications

Tramadol 25 mg every four hours as needed for pain; lisinopril 10 mg daily; Lipitor 10 mg daily; Aggrenox 20/200 ER twice a day; vitamin D 5000 units daily

Allergies

NKDA

Review of Systems

General: Good energy level
Integumentary: No itching or rashes
HEENT: No history of head injury or headaches, no corrective lenses, denies eye pain, no excessive tearing, blurring, or change in vision; no tinnitus or vertigo; denies frequent colds, hay fever, or sinus problems
Neck: No lumps, goiters, or pain
Respiratory: Denies shortness of breath; no paroxysmal nocturnal dyspnea
Cardiovascular: No chest pain, no shortness of breath with normal activity. No excessive bruising, no history of transfusions.
Gastrointestinal: No nausea, vomiting, constipation, or diarrhea; denies belching, bloating, and black or clay-colored stools
Genitourinary: As in History of Present Illness, earlier in this case study
Extremities: No joint pains or swelling
Neurological: No seizures; denies numbness, paresthesias, or weakness
Endocrine: No polyuria, polyphagia, polydipsia; temperature tolerances good

Physical Examination

Vital signs: Temperature 98°F; pulse 76 bpm; respirations 18/min; BP 140/74 mm Hg
Height: 5 ft 6 in; *Weight:* 167 lb; *BMI:* 27.0

General: Caucasian female in no apparent distress; appears stated age

HEENT: Normocephalic without masses or lesions; pupils equal, round, and reactive to light; EOMI; fundi benign; nares patent and noninjected; throat without redness or lesions

Neck: Supple without thyromegaly or adenopathy

Thorax: CTAP

Heart: RRR without murmurs, rubs, or gallops

Abdominal/gastrointestinal: No HSM; abdomen soft, nontender; bowel sounds normoactive; rectal without masses; stool brown, guaiac negative; normal sphincter tone

Genitourinary: External without lesions, vaginal mucosa pink with mild atrophy, cervix without gross lesions, no discharge noted, uterus is absent, no adnexal tenderness; grade 3 cystocele; rectocele 1+

Extremities: Range of motion functionally intact; no cyanosis, clubbing, or edema

Neurological: Reflexes 2+ at Achilles, patellar, biceps, triceps, and brachioradialis; no Babinski reflexes present

Laboratory Results:

All tests performed one week ago (Table 3-1).

TABLE 3-1	Laboratory Test Results for Polly Latour	
COMPLETE BLOOD COUNT		
	Result	Normal Range
WBC	4.6	4.5–10.8
RBC	4.45	4.20–5.4
Hgb	11.7	12.0–16.0
Hct	36.6	37.0–47.0
MCV	98.3	81.0–99.0
MCH	31.2	27.0–32.0
MCHC	33.4	32.0–36.0
RDW	16.2	11.0–16.0
Platelets	221	150–450
Segments	58	50–65
Lymphocytes	29	25–45
Monocytes	9	0–10
Eos	4	0–4

CHEMISTRY PROFILE		
	Result	Normal Range
FBS	130	60–100
BUN	20	8–28
Creatinine	1.0	0.5–1.5
Sodium	137	135–145
Potassium	4.3	3.5–5.5
Chloride	104	95–105
Albumin	3.8	4.0–6.0
Total protein	6.1	6.5–8.0
Alk phos	100	30–120
ALT	48	0–40
AST	58	0–40
LDH	134	50–150
Calcium	9.0	8.8–10.2
GGT	29	0–30

continued

CHEMISTRY PROFILE—cont'd		
	Result	Normal Range
Magnesium	1.6	1.6–2.4
Bilirubin	0.7	0.1–1.0
Conjugated bilirubin	0.1	0.0–0.2
Iron	80	60–160
Uric acid	6.3	2.0–7.0
Hgb A1C	7.2	

LIPID PROFILE		
	Results	Normal Range
Total cholesterol	153	<200
HDL	41	30-60
LDL	92	≤130
Triglycerides	99	≤150
Risk ratio	3.73	≤4.0

URINALYSIS		
	Results	Normal Range
Color	Yellow	
Character	Clear	
s.g.	1.015	1.005-1.025
pH	5.5	4.5-8
Glucose	Neg	
Protein	Neg	
Nitrite	Neg	
WBCs	3–5	≤2-5
RBCs	3–5	≤2
Epi cells	15	≤15-20
Crystals	None	

After reviewing the case and the Grading Criteria in Appendix A, jot down your notes or preliminary answers in the spaces provided below. When you are ready to submit your answers for grading (if you are working with an instructor) and reflective feedback to help you evaluate your answers, go to http://www.evolve.elsevier.com/Cappiello/ to complete this case.

Learning Issues

Before identifying your recommended Assessment and Plan, identify any learning issues that you believe are important for you to explore about this case:

Assessment

Please indicate the problems or issues you have identified that will guide your care (preferably in list form):

Plan

Please list your plans for addressing each of the problems or issues in your assessment:

Case 4

Jenilee Heidemann

Age 20 years

Opening Scenario

A 20-year-old woman makes an appointment to see you for pregnancy-related symptoms. This is her first visit with you.

History of Present Illness

"I have been having mild nausea for the past week and I thought I had some sort of bug. Then yesterday morning I vomited and it made me feel much better. I had started to wonder if I was pregnant, so I did a home pregnancy test and it was positive.

"I transferred to our state university because I couldn't afford private college tuition anymore. I got here a week ago to settle into my apartment before classes start next week. I'm not signed up for College Health Services yet. My boyfriend, Mike, and I have been together for eight months but I had sort of been thinking our relationship might not last now that we are 100 miles apart. I was OK with that as he is probably not the guy I want to spend the rest of my life with. Then this happens....

"I called him last night to tell him about the pregnancy test. He was shocked but he did say he would support me in whatever decision I make. I can't see how he could possibly want to be a father and raise a child at this point in his life—he really wants to finish college. But he wouldn't tell me his gut feelings one way or the other.

"I feel so alone with this decision. I'm not really in touch with my old high school friends who are at this university. My parents are great, but I don't feel like I can share this decision with them. It doesn't seem fair to ask them for financial help with raising a child—they're already struggling to help pay for college for my sister and me. I haven't talked with my sister about this but I might."

Medical History

G0P0. Negative for chronic illnesses. No hospitalizations or surgery. No mental illness, depression, or anxiety. Up-to-date on all immunizations, including HPV.

Menstrual History: Menarche at age 15 and irregular. Four to six periods per year, usually lasting four to five days. Flow: Average amount; she occasionally takes ibuprofen for mild cramping. Her last menstrual period (LMP) was eight weeks ago, but she is not worried because this is not unusual.

Contraceptive history: Currently condoms, consistent use. Chose because of protection against sexually transmitted diseases (STDs) and pregnancy. Used oral contraceptives for two years but often forgot to take, so stopped and has been using condoms for the past year.

Family Medical History

Mother: 43 years old (A&W)
Father: 45 years old, (HTN, started medication recently)
Sister: 23 years old (A&W)

Social History

Nonsmoker. Alcohol: Three or four drinks on the weekend, more on nights during the summer. Denies drug use. Good relationship with family.

Medications

None

Allergies

NKDA

Review of Systems

General: Good energy level if obtains enough sleep
Integumentary: No rashes, itching, or lesions
Respiratory: Denies shortness of breath (SOB), paroxysmal nocturnal dyspnea (PND)
Cardiovascular: Denies chest pain, SOB, palpitations
Gastrointestinal: Some nausea with food odors for past week; no vomiting; no heartburn, abdominal pain, diarrhea, constipation, rectal bleeding, black or clay-colored stools; no history of hepatitis
Genitourinary: No history of sexually transmitted infections, vaginitis, UTIs; no spotting between periods or bleeding after intercourse, vaginal discharge/itching, pelvic pain, pain with intercourse, or dysuria; no unusual cramping in the past few weeks
Neurological: No seizures, fainting, weakness, numbness
Endocrine: No polydipsia, urinating more frequently

After reviewing the case and the Grading Criteria in Appendix A, jot down your notes or preliminary answers in the spaces provided below. When you are ready to submit your answers for grading (if you are working with an instructor) and reflective feedback to help you evaluate your answers, go to http://www.evolve.elsevier.com/Cappiello/ to complete this case.

Learning Issues

Before identifying your recommended Assessment and Plan, identify any learning issues that you believe are important for you to explore about this case:

Assessment

Please indicate the problems or issues you have identified that will guide your care (preferably in list form):

Plan

Please list your plans for addressing each of the problems or issues in your assessment:

Case 5

Kate Smith
Age 29 years

Opening Scenario

Kate Smith is a 29-year-old woman scheduled for an episodic visit with a complaint of painful urination. This is her first visit to your practice.

History of Present Illness

"I'm having difficulty urinating. I had something like this five years ago and it was a bladder infection. I have been urinating more often, have burning with urination, and sometimes feel like I have to urinate but then nothing comes out. This started yesterday, woke me during the night, and has made me very uncomfortable this morning. I'm also having some sharp pain right above my pubic area. I took one ibuprofen last night and this morning, but it didn't help all that much."

Medical History

G0P0 with last menstrual period (LMP) one week ago. Reported history of one previous urinary tract infection (UTI), no history of kidney infections or renal calculi. No history of major medical problems. Tonsillectomy and adenoidectomy as child. No other hospitalizations. Reports gynecological examination, Papanicolaou (Pap) testing, and sexually transmitted infection (STI) screen one year ago with previous provider. Completed childhood immunizations. Tdap five years ago. Completed human papillomavirus (HPV) series.

Family Medical History

Mother: 47 years old (A&W)
Father: 50 years old (hypertension)
Siblings: Two brothers, 23 and 20 years old (A&W)

Social History

Moved three months ago to begin graduate school. Single, lives with a female room-mate. Two male sexual partners in the past year. Reports condom use most of the time, denies unprotected sex since her LMP.

Medications

Occasional ibuprofen: 200 mg tablets
Oral contraceptives: Loestrin 24 Fe

Allergies

NKDA

Review of Systems

General: Feels well besides urinary symptoms; no fever or fatigue
Gastrointestinal: No nausea, vomiting, abdominal pain, constipation, or diarrhea
Genitourinary: Urinary symptoms as described previously; no abnormal bleeding, vaginal discharge/itching, or lesions; she is happy with birth control pills, takes consistently

Physical Examination

Vital signs: Temperature 98.4° F; pulse 70 bpm; respirations 16/min; BP 110/60 mm Hg BMI: 27
General: Healthy-appearing female in no acute distress
Abdomen: Slight tenderness to palpation in suprapubic area; abdomen soft without masses; no costovertebral angle (CVA) tenderness
Pelvic: Deferred
In-office laboratory results: Urine dipstick test (Table 5-1)

TABLE 5-1	Urine Dipstick Test for Kate Smith
Test	**Result**
Color	Yellow
Appearance	Cloudy
Glucose	Negative
Ketones	Negative
Blood	Small
Protein	Trace
Leukocytes	Moderate
Nitrites	Negative

After reviewing the case and the Grading Criteria in Appendix A, jot down your notes or preliminary answers in the spaces provided below. When you are ready to submit your answers for grading (if you are working with an instructor) and reflective feedback to help you evaluate your answers, go to **http://www.evolve.elsevier.com/Cappiello/** to complete this case.

Learning Issues

Before identifying your recommended Assessment and Plan, identify any learning issues that you believe are important for you to explore about this case:

Assessment

Please indicate the problems or issues you have identified that will guide your care (preferably in list form):

Continued

Plan

Please list your plans for addressing each of the problems or issues in your assessment:

Case 6

Francis Coulter
Age 32 years

Opening Scenario

Francis Coulter is a 32-year-old male here for an episodic visit with a complaint of head congestion. He has been seen in your practice for the past two years.

History of Present Illness

"I have had a cough and runny nose for over two weeks. About a week ago I developed a headache and started blowing thick, yellow-green mucus out of my nose. Bending over seems to make the headache worse. Acetaminophen improves the headache but doesn't take it away. I've also been using pseudoephedrine 30 mg, two tablets every 12 hours with little relief." The patient denies tooth pain or pain with mastication.

Medical History

Seen here for a physical examination one year ago with no positive findings. No history of surgery, hospitalizations, coronary artery disease, hypertension, or diabetes.

Social History

Nonsmoker, rare alcohol (less than three drinks a month). Works as a junior high school science teacher.

Medications

Pseudoephedrine hydrochloride: 60 mg every 12 hours for the past three days
Cough drops for sore throat
Acetaminophen: 1000 mg every four hours as needed for headache

Allergies

NKDA

Review of Systems

HEENT: Mild pain with swallowing; denies ear pain or discharge; no tinnitus or vertigo; describes purulent nasal discharge; has no history of allergies or allergic rhinitis; denies a history of frequent colds, hay fever, sinus problems; denies tooth pain
Cardiovascular: Denies chest pain
Respiratory: No shortness of breath or asthma; nonproductive cough
Abdominal/Gastrointestinal: No symptoms of nausea, vomiting, diarrhea
Neurological: Dull frontal headache, worse with bending over, for a week (4 on scale of 1 to 10)

Physical Examination

Vital signs: Temperature 99.6° F; pulse 72 bpm; respirations 16/min; BP 126/82 mm Hg
HEENT: Tenderness to palpation over frontal area R>L, no maxillary tenderness; tympanic membranes dull but not red, landmarks visible; nasal mucosa erythematous, boggy turbinates, no polyps noted; purulent yellow-greenish nasal discharge; pharynx: Erythematous, cobbled appearance; no obvious dental disease; submaxillary nodes enlarged; no cervical adenopathy
Heart: Regular rate and rhythm; no murmurs, rubs, or gallops
Lungs: Clear to auscultation

After reviewing the case and the Grading Criteria in Appendix A, jot down your notes or preliminary answers in the spaces provided below. When you are ready to submit your answers for grading (if you are working with an instructor) and reflective feedback to help you evaluate your answers, go to **http://www.evolve.elsevier.com/Cappiello/** to complete this case.

Learning Issues

Before identifying your recommended Assessment and Plan, identify any learning issues that you believe are important for you to explore about this case:

Assessment

Please indicate the problems or issues you have identified that will guide your care (preferably in list form):

Plan

Please list your plans for addressing each of the problems or issues in your assessment:

Case 7

Lianne Pierce
Age 6 years

Opening Scenario

Lianne Pierce is a 6-year-old Latina girl on your schedule for rash with sore throat and fever. Her mother is present and appears to be in her late twenties. Lianne is sitting quietly on the examination table.

History of Present Illness

(Obtained from mother)
"Lianne has been sick for about four days. It started with a headache, but she sometimes complains of a headache when she is tired so I didn't think much of it. Then she got a sore throat two to three days ago. Now she feels warm (but I couldn't find my thermometer because we just moved) and has this rash that started yesterday, so I thought I should bring her in. The rash came on about this time yesterday, and it has not really changed since it started. She says the rash is just a little itchy. She says her tummy hurts sometimes."

Lianne's mother has made no changes in laundry detergent, no new clothing, and no new foods or seafood in the past week. Denies known exposure to anyone with chickenpox or any other rash. You have not seen any similar cases recently in your practice. Lianne has no history of similar rashes or upper respiratory infections (URIs).

Medical History

Growth percentiles within normal limits on previous visits. Milestones all within normal limits on previous visits. No chronic illnesses, no history of surgical procedures. Immunization record is shown in Table 7-1.

TABLE 7-1   Immunization Record for Lianne Pierce

Vaccine	Date	Initials	Notes	Vaccine	Date	Initials	Notes
DTap	2 mo	MDO		MMR	5 yr	KJ	
DTap	4 mo	KJ		HBV	Birth		Hospital
DTap	6 mo	MDO		HBV	3 mo	KJ	
DTap	18 mo	MDO		HBV	9 mo	KJ	
DTap	5 yr	KJ		HAV	4 yr	MDO	
Influenza IIV	12 mo	KJ		HAV	5 yr	MDO	
Influenza IIV	2 yr	KJ		Hib	2 mo	MDO	
Influenza LAIV	3 yr	MDO		Hib	4 mo	KJ	
Influenza LAIV	4 yr	MDO		Hib	6 mo	MDO	
Influenza LAIV	5 yr	MDO		Hib	18 mo	MDO	
Influenza LAIV	6 yr	MDO		Pneumo 13	2 mo	KJ	
IPV	2 mo	MDO		Pneumo 13	4 mo	KJ	
IPV	4 mo	KJ		Pneumo 13	6 mo	KJ	
IPV	18 mo	MDO		Pneumo 13	18 mo	KJ	
IPV	5 yr	MDO		Varicella	12 mo	KJ	
OPV	5 yr	KJ		Varicella	5 yr	MDO	
MMR	13 mo	KJ					

Family Medical History

MGM: 51 years old (A&W)
MGF: 50 years old (high cholesterol)
PGM: 48 years old (breast cancer)
PGF: 50 years old (A&W)
Mother: 27 years old (A&W)
Father: 27 years old (A&W)
Brother: 8 years old (A&W)

Social History

Lives with mother. Spends every other weekend with father about one-half hour away. Mother works in an accounting firm. Father is an administrator of a public social service agency. Parents have been divorced about two years. In first grade; doing well. Sleeps well. No behavioral problems.

Medications

No prescription medications; no over-the-counter medications

Allergies

NKDA

Review of Systems

General: Fatigue since onset of symptoms; diminished appetite with onset of sore throat; sleep disturbed last night due to complaint of sore throat; denies weight changes

Integumentary: 24-hour history of raised pink pruritic rash on abdomen, back, upper legs; denies chronic or recurrent rashes

HEENT: Cold symptoms about two to three times a year; denies current or chronic nasal or sinus congestion, ear pressure or pain, hearing loss; see History of Present Illness earlier in this case

Neck: Tender lymph glands bilateral since onset of sore throat; denies stiffness

Respiratory: Denies cough, shortness of breath, wheeze

Cardiovascular: Denies cyanosis, dizziness, swelling of extremities

Gastrointestinal: Denies vomiting, constipation, or diarrhea

Genitourinary: Denies pain with urination, dark color or foul odor to urine; denies incontinence

Musculoskeletal: Denies joint pain, swelling; denies muscle aches

Neurological: Intermittent mild headache for four days; denies problem concentrating, lethargy, seizures

Physical Examination

Vital signs: Temperature 100.8° F (oral); pulse 96 bpm; respirations 26/min

Height: 46 in (same as at 6-year checkup five weeks ago); *weight:* 42 lb (weight at 6-year checkup five weeks ago was 41.5 lb)

General: Well nourished, well developed; in no acute distress. Appetite diminished but drinking normal amounts of liquids.

Nutritional: Appetite diminished but drinking normal amounts

Skin: Confluent maculopapular, blanching rash predominantly on anterior and posterior trunk and thighs; texture of rash consistent with sandpaper quality; no pustules, vesicles; no desquamation noted; bright red skin in underarm, elbow, and groin creases

HEENT: Normocephalic without masses or lesions; conjunctiva noninjected; pupils equal, round, and reactive to light; extraocular movements intact; nares patent and noninjected; posterior pharynx erythematous; tonsils 1+ with purulent exudate on right tonsil; mild petechiae on soft palate, none on uvula; teeth in good repair; tongue red with bumps, and in the midline; tympanic membranes (TMs) slightly dull and retracted, cone of light slightly diffused, TMs mobile

Neck: Supple without thyromegaly; a few mildly tender, minimally enlarged less than 1 cm, anterior cervical nodes palpable; no posterior or occipital nodes palpable

Thorax: Clear to auscultation and percussion; no adventitious sounds

Heart: Regular rate and rhythm; no murmurs, rubs, or gallops

Abdomen/Gastrointestinal: No hepatosplenomegaly; abdomen soft, nontender without guarding or rebound; bowel sounds normoactive

Peripheral vascular: Brachial and femoral pulses 2+ bilaterally; no edema present

Extremities: Full range of motion of hips/knees/ankles; joints smooth, nontender

Neurological: Alert and moving easily in examination room, developmentally appropriate behavior and responses.

Diagnostics: Rapid antigen detection test (RADT) for group A streptococci: Positive

---

After reviewing the case and the Grading Criteria in Appendix A, jot down your notes or preliminary answers in the spaces provided below. When you are ready to submit your answers for grading (if you are working with an instructor) and reflective feedback to help you evaluate your answers, go to **http://www.evolve.elsevier.com/Cappiello/** to complete this case.

Learning Issues

Before identifying your recommended Assessment and Plan, identify any learning issues that you believe are important for you to explore about this case:

Assessment

Please indicate the problems or issues you have identified that will guide your care (preferably in list form):

Plan

Please list your plans for addressing each of the problems or issues in your assessment:

Case 8

Wendy Raymond
Age 38 years

Opening Scenario

Wendy Raymond is a 38-year-old woman who is new to this practice. Her primary complaint today is her problems with migraine headaches.

History of Present Illness

"I have had migraines for about 10 years. I have about four to five per month, and they are very severe. I have nausea and occasional vomiting. I have the sensation of flashing lights in my eyes before I get the headache. The headaches are more often on the right than left. They seem to come most frequently on weekends. They last about 6 to 8 hours, are improved by going into a dark room and lying down with a cool cloth on my forehead. I haven't sought treatment before because I hate coming into an office and I've just been too busy. I finally decided that I needed to do something now because I've been missing family events and the headaches seem to be getting more frequent. I have tried acetaminophen 1000 mg every 4 hours when I get a headache, but it has minimal effect. I have not noticed particular foods or activities that cause my headaches. I have no history of head trauma."

Medical History

Tonsillectomy and adenoidectomy as a child and endometriosis diagnosed at age 19. No other hospitalizations or injuries.

Family Medical History

MGM: 82 years old (mild arthritis)
MGF: Deceased at age 71 (heart attack)
PGM: Deceased at age 64 (Alzheimer's disease)
PGF: Deceased at age 79 (stroke)
Mother: 63 years old (mild HTN)

Father: 65 years old (chronic obstructive pulmonary disease; occasionally has problems with his eyes "going out of focus")

Siblings: Two sisters 35 and 41 years old (A&W)

Social History

Married for 17 years. Two children, 8 and 10 years old. Works as a fourth-grade teacher. Never smoked. Alcohol very rarely (only for a toast at a wedding). Has one cup of regular coffee each morning. Denies other caffeine intake.

Medications

Acetaminophen: 1000 mg every 4 hours (when she gets a headache) for three to four doses

Allergies

NKDA

Review of Systems

General: Overall health good

Integumentary: No itching or rashes or lesions

HEENT: No history of head injury; no corrective lenses; denies eye pain, excessive tearing, blurring, or change in vision; no tinnitus or vertigo; denies frequent colds, hay fever, or sinus problems; headaches as noted under History of Present Illness

Neck: No lumps, goiters, or pain

Thorax: Denies shortness of breath, paroxysmal nocturnal dyspnea

Cardiovascular: No chest pain, no shortness of breath with normal activity, no palpitations. No excessive bruising; no history of transfusions

Hematological: No excessive bruising; no history of transfusions

Gastrointestinal: No nausea, vomiting, constipation, or diarrhea; denies belching, bloating, reflux, and black or clay-colored stools

Genitourinary: No dysuria; frequency; hormonal IUD × 3 years; history of endometriosis followed by her gynecologist, but she does not currently perceive it to be a problem because she started the hormonal IUD and has no menses; G2P2

Musculoskeletal: No joint pains or swelling

Neurological: No seizures, no numbness or tingling, no falls or dizziness

Endocrine: No polyuria, polyphagia, polydipsia; temperature tolerances good, no unexplained weight gain or loss

Physical Examination

Vital signs: Temperature 98.0° F; pulse 76 bpm; respirations 18/min, BP 120/74 mm Hg

Height: 5 ft 6 in; *weight:* 127 lb

General: Well nourished, well developed; in no acute distress; appears stated age

HEENT: Normocephalic without masses or lesions; pupils equal, round, and reactive to light; extraocular movements intact; fundi no AV narrowing or nicking, no papilledema, nares patent and mucosa noninjected; throat without erythema or lesions; no tenderness on temporal palpation or on sinus percussion/palpation; no deviation or clicks on mandibular opening; teeth in good repair

Neck: Supple without thyromegaly or adenopathy

Heart: Regular rate and rhythm; no murmurs, rubs, or gallops

Lungs: Clear to auscultation and percussion

Abdomen: No hepatosplenomegaly; abdomen soft, nontender, no masses

Extremities: Range of motion functionally intact; no cyanosis, clubbing, or edema

Neurological: Reflexes 2+ at Achilles, patellar, biceps, triceps, and brachioradialis; negative Babinski; cranial nerves 2 to 12 intact; negative Romberg; point-to-point movements intact; motor and sensory findings normal and symmetrical

After reviewing the case and the Grading Criteria in Appendix A, jot down your notes or preliminary answers in the spaces provided below. When you are ready to submit your answers for grading (if you are working with an instructor) and reflective feedback to help you evaluate your answers, go to **http://www.evolve.elsevier.com/Cappiello/** to complete this case.

Learning Issues

Before identifying your recommended Assessment and Plan, identify any learning issues that you believe are important for you to explore about this case:

Continued

Assessment

Please indicate the problems or issues you have identified that will guide your care (preferably in list form):

Plan

Please list your plans for addressing each of the problems or issues in your assessment:

Case 9

Liu Lee
Age 24 years

Opening Scenario

Liu Lee is a 24-year-old woman scheduled for an acute visit for unprotected coitus after a birth control failure. Her last visit with you was nine months ago for an annual gynecological examination. She tells you she has heard she could buy the "morning after pill" over the counter but she was not sure where to go or if all pharmacies would sell this to her without a prescription. She is also worried about the cost because her friend told her the pill could cost up to $60. As a graduate student she is on a limited budget and she is hoping that if she has a prescription, her insurance will cover the cost.

History of Present Illness

"My boyfriend and I have been using condoms for birth control. The condom broke last night, and my period was two weeks ago. I don't want to be pregnant because I am a graduate student in a doctoral program. I have at least three years of school ahead of me. Is there anything I can do at this point to prevent a pregnancy?"

Medical History

A review of her records shows that her last gynecological examination was nine months ago with a negative examination and negative Pap smear; G0P0; healthy, overweight female with regular 27- to 28-day cycles. No history of hospitalizations or surgeries. All immunizations up to date, including hepatitis B. Seen three months ago for an uncomplicated upper respiratory infection.

Family Medical History

MGM: 70 years old (A&W)
MGF: 70 years old (A&W)
PGM: 73 years old (type 2 DM)
PGF: Deceased at age 35 (accident)

Mother: 44 years old (A&W)
Father: 48 years old (high cholesterol)
Sister: 18 years old (A&W)

Social History

Has a steady boyfriend for the past two years whom she plans to marry in the future. At some point they would like to have a family. Smokes one-half pack per day. Denies drug use. States consumption of one glass of wine with dinner three times a week. Denies domestic violence.

Medications

None

Allergies

NKDA

Review of Systems

General: Feels healthy but often fatigued and stressed from demands of school; sleeps five to six hours per night; states she requires more sleep than this, but needs the time for studying

HEENT: States no further upper respiratory symptoms since her visit three months ago; has not made any progress in decreasing smoking; states that the stress of graduate school makes smoking cessation difficult; wants to work on quitting in the summer because she will not attend summer school this year; thinks this will lower her stress level and, in addition, the restaurant where she will work as a waitress is a smoke-free environment

Respiratory: Denies chest pain, shortness of breath, asthma, or any breathing difficulties

Breasts: No history of masses, skin changes, nipple discharge

Gastrointestinal: Denies heartburn, nausea and vomiting, abdominal pain, constipation, diarrhea, changes in bowel habits, rectal bleeding; no history of hepatitis or liver disease

Genitourinary: No complaints of pelvic pain or abnormal vaginal bleeding; no history of kidney disease, urinary tract infections

Physical Examination

Vital signs: Temperature 98.0° F; pulse 68 bpm; respirations 16/min; BP 110/70 mm Hg

Height: 5 ft 2 in; *weight:* 160 lb; *BMI:* 29.3

No other physical examination performed today.

After reviewing the case and the Grading Criteria in Appendix A, jot down your notes or preliminary answers in the spaces provided below. When you are ready to submit your answers for grading (if you are working with an instructor) and reflective feedback to help you evaluate your answers, go to **http://www.evolve.elsevier.com/Cappiello/** to complete this case.

Learning Issues

Before identifying your recommended Assessment and Plan, identify any learning issues that you believe are important for you to explore about this case:

Assessment

Please indicate the problems or issues you have identified that will guide your care (preferably in list form):

Plan

Please list your plans for addressing each of the problems or issues in your assessment:

Case 10

Amber Jackson

Age 20 weeks

Opening Scenario

Amber Jackson is a 20-week-old female in your office for a four-month WCC. Both parents are present.

History of Present Illness

(Obtained from mother)

"Amber is here for her well-child check and her immunizations. She is a great baby and doesn't cry much. We do have some concerns about constipation. What should we be giving her for formula? Starting two weeks ago she was getting constipated, so we switched her to low-iron formula. We have been giving her one oz of prune juice mixed with 1 oz of water when she seems constipated. It seems to work and we have given this three times over the last two weeks. Is that okay? Also, she is still up twice a night. How much longer is that going to last?"

Medical History

Normal spontaneous vaginal delivery at term. Developmental milestones all within normal limits on previous visit. Immunization record is shown in Table 10-1. Growth is shown in Table 10-2.

Family Medical History

MGM: 44 years old (A&W)
MGF: 46 years old (A&W)
PGM: 53 years old (HTN, DM)
PGF: 58 years old (prostate cancer)
Mother: 27 years old (A&W)
Father: 37 years old (A&W)

TABLE 10-1	Immunization Record for Amber Jackson		
Vaccine	Date	Initials	Notes
Hep B #1	1 day	KN	
Hep B #2	2 mo	MDO	
Hep B #3			
RV #1			
RV #2			
RV #3			
DTaP #1	2 mo	MDO	Pentacel
DTaP #2			
DTaP #3			
DTaP #4			
DTap #5			
Hib #1	2 mo	MDO	Pentacel
Hib #2			
Hib #3			
Hib #4			
PCV #1	2 mo	MDO	
PCV #2			
PCV #3			
PCV #4			
IPV #1	2 mo	MDO	Pentacel
IPV #2			
IPV #3			
IPV #4			
Influenza			

TABLE 10-2	Growth of Amber Jackson		
Measure	Age	Result	Percentile
Length	Birth	19 in	33%
	2 wk	19½ in	28%
	2 mo	22½ in	34%
	4 mo	24 in	26%
Weight	Birth	6 lb, 12 oz	25%
	2 wk	7 lb	22%
	2 mo	11 lb	36%
	4 mo	13 lb, 8 oz	34%
Head circumference	Birth	13½ in	39%
	2 wk	13½ in	18%
	2 mo	15¼ in	31%
	4 mo	16 in	29%

Social History

Lives with both parents in an apartment. Father works as a truck driver and frequently travels. Mother stays with child at home. No siblings. Mother is from the Philippines and of small stature (4 ft 11 in, 105 lb). Mother has been in this country for about five years. No local family, some local friends.

Medications

None

Allergies

NKDA

Review of Systems

(Obtained from mother)
General: Good energy level, no fevers, in good general health
Integumentary: No itching, lesions, or rashes

HEENT: Mild transient congestion after feeding; no difficulty swallowing; no concerns about hearing or vision; not pulling at ears

Respiratory: Denies apnea, shortness of breath, and cough

Cardiovascular: No cyanosis, diaphoresis

Gastrointestinal: No vomiting or diarrhea; usually two soft, brown bowel movements (BMs) per day until two weeks ago, then had two days without BMs after which formula was changed; returned to daily BM—strains with BMs at times

Genitourinary: No odor to urine; six to seven wet diapers per day

Musculoskeletal: Moves all extremities routinely

Neurological: No seizures, alert, smiles spontaneously

Physical Examination

Vital signs: Temperature 98.0° F; pulse 106 bpm; respirations 24/min

General: Well nourished, well developed; in no acute distress; smiling during examination

HEENT: Normocephalic without masses or lesions; posterior fontanel closed, anterior fontanel palpable, soft, and flat; pupils equal, round, and reactive to light, positive red reflex; tracks with eyes, nares patent and noninjected; posterior pharynx without redness or lesions; tympanic membranes (TMs) noninjected, crisp cone of light, TMs mobile

Neck: Supple, no abnormal adenopathy

Thorax: Clear to auscultation and percussion

Heart: Regular rate and rhythm; no murmurs, rubs, or gallops

Gastrointestinal: Abdomen soft, nontender; no hepatosplenomegaly

Neurological: No head lag when pulled to a sitting position; rolls to side easily, pulls up to elbows; tracks object with eyes, babbling

Extremities: Femoral pulses 2+; full range of motion of hips; no cyanosis, clubbing, or edema

Nutrition: Breastfeeding until three weeks ago; started on Similac and then switched to low-iron Similac; taking 4- to 5-oz bottles every four to five hours for 24 to 30 oz of formula per day; has not yet had cereal or other solid food

Developmental: Reports infant is smiling, babbling, able to hold head erect, can self-soothe, indicates pleasure/displeasure; rolls to side and from front to back; reaches for objects, puts hands in mouth, and pulls up to elbows

After reviewing the case and the Grading Criteria in Appendix A, jot down your notes or preliminary answers in the spaces provided below. When you are ready to submit your answers for grading (if you are working with an instructor) and reflective feedback to help you evaluate your answers, go to **http://www.evolve.elsevier.com/Cappiello/** to complete this case.

Learning Issues

Before identifying your recommended Assessment and Plan, identify any learning issues that you believe are important for you to explore about this case:

Assessment

Please indicate the problems or issues you have identified that will guide your care (preferably in list form):

Plan

Please list your plans for addressing each of the problems or issues in your assessment:

Case 11

11:30 AM
M'Tango Bali
Age 45 years

Opening Scenario

M'Tango Bali is a 45-year-old professor from a nearby university who is planning to spend a month in Belize working on an educational project and doing research. He makes an appointment for a pretravel consultation. This is his first visit to your office.

History of Present Illness

"I plan to spend time in rural areas, living and working with people in the smaller villages. I will be living in people's homes and eating meals with them some of the time. I want to know what I need for shots and how to stay healthy on my trip. My field of study is education. I plan to spend much of my time working in schools. I leave in one month."

Medical History

Generally healthy. No hospitalizations or surgeries. Has had problems with cholesterol and has been on lovastatin for the past eight months. Last physical examination: 1½ years ago. Immunizations: Unsure of last tetanus, thinks it was 20 years ago when he went to college. Does not think he had immunizations for hepatitis A or B.

Family Medical History

MGM: Deceased at age 95 (osteoarthritis)
MGF: Deceased at age 71 (lung cancer)
PGM: Deceased at age 80 (natural causes)
PGF: Deceased at age 77 (MI)
Mother: 70 years old (A&W)
Father: Deceased at age 68 (MI)
One sister, one brother: 41, 37 years old (A&W)

Social History

Born in Tanzania and moved to the United States at age five Divorced for two years. Two children in high school who live with their mother. Nonsmoker. Moved here five months ago to take a position at the university. Works out at a gym two to three times a week, plus plays racquetball twice a week. Sleeps seven hours per night.

Medications

Lovastatin: 20 mg daily
Ibuprofen: 400 mg as needed for joint discomfort

Allergies

NKDA

Review of Systems

General: Denies appetite or weight changes; no unusual fatigue; no prior reactions to vaccines

HEENT: Denies headaches, blurry vision; wears glasses for reading; no complaints of hearing loss; mild seasonal hay fever; no history of asthma; no problems with frequent colds, sore throats

Cardiovascular: Denies chest pain; no history of palpitations, murmurs, hypertension; states cholesterol was elevated, cannot remember exact figures; worked on diet and exercise but the numbers did not change much; put on lovastatin eight months ago; had normal liver function tests (LFTs) after four weeks on medication

Respiratory: No complaints of shortness of breath, dyspnea, cough; no history of bronchitis or asthma

Gastrointestinal: Good appetite; trying a low-carbohydrate diet since diagnosed with high cholesterol 1½ years ago but eats out often and finds it difficult to make good choices; no heartburn, ulcer, diarrhea, constipation; no history of exposure to hepatitis

Genitourinary: No problems with urination; no history of kidney problems; denies sexual problems

Musculoskeletal: Right knee bothers him periodically but able to play racquetball and exercise without problems

Neurological: No history of seizures, weakness, dizziness, syncope; no history of depression, psychiatric disorders

Physical Examination

Vital signs: Temperature 98.2° F; pulse 72 bpm; respirations 16/min; BP 136/84 mm Hg

Height: 5 ft 11 in; *weight:* 200 lb *BMI:* 28

General: Healthy male who appears his stated age No tenderness to palpation to sinus area, no nasal discharge, good dentition, pharynx without redness, tympanic membranes clear, no lymphadenopathy.

Heart: Regular rate and rhythm; no murmurs, rubs HEENT, or gallops

Lungs: Clear to auscultation

Extremities: Right knee: No bruising, swelling, erythema; no point tenderness, but client points to right medial aspect of the knee as area of aching and swelling after vigorous, prolonged physical activity; normal range of motion; no ballottement; negative bulge sign; negative McMurray and drawer tests (anterior and posterior); no cyanosis, clubbing, or edema; left knee: No bruising, swelling, erythema, tenderness

Neurological: Muscle strength testing: 5/5 of both lower extremities; deep tendon reflexes (biceps, triceps, patellar, ankle) 2+

After reviewing the case and the Grading Criteria in Appendix A, jot down your notes or preliminary answers in the spaces provided below. When you are ready to submit your answers for grading (if you are working with an instructor) and reflective feedback to help you evaluate your answers, go to **http://www.evolve.elsevier.com/Cappiello/** to complete this case.

Learning Issues

Before identifying your recommended Assessment and Plan, identify any learning issues that you believe are important for you to explore about this case:

Continued

Assessment

Please indicate the problems or issues you have identified that will guide your care (preferably in list form):

Plan

Please list your plans for addressing each of the problems or issues in your assessment:

Case 12

Martha Krauntz

Age 35 years

Opening Scenario

Martha Krauntz is a 35-year-old woman scheduled for an episodic visit for cold symptoms. She was seen in your office five years ago. Since then, she has been followed by her women's health nurse practitioner (NP).

History of Present Illness

"I've had this cold for three to four days. My kids have it also. I'm going to be traveling on an airplane in two days and I'm worried about how I'll feel when flying. When I flew a few years ago, my ears really hurt and I didn't have a cold then. I've been taking some acetaminophen and Sudafed with some relief. I've been reading about *Echinacea* and vitamin C. Do you think either would help? How much should I take?" The patient complains of copious, clear to yellow nasal discharge, head stuffiness, sneezing, mild cough, and occasional mild headache "all over." She denies fever, frontal or maxillary pain, ear pain, or dental pain. She has been able to work and attend all other activities without interruption.

Medical History

Healthy individual. Two hospitalizations in the past four years related to uncomplicated childbirth. No surgeries. No major medical problems or chronic disease.

Family Medical History

Mother: Hypothyroidism
Father: Skin cancer, history of prostate cancer, and HTN
Two sisters: A&W, one with depression

Social History

Nonsmoker. Lives with husband and two children, ages 2 and 4. Works part-time as store clerk. Attends Zumba classes three times per week and volunteers at preschool program. Consumes one to two glasses of wine weekly.

Medications

Acetaminophen: 650 mg every four hours as needed for fever or mild pain
Pseudoephedrine hydrochloride: Sustained release, 120 mg, one tablet every 12 hours for two days
Levonorgestrel: 52 mg intrauterine device (IUD)
Multivitamin: One tablet daily

Allergies

NKDA

Review of Systems

General: No chills, fever, body aches
HEENT: No history of environmental allergies or asthma; has 1 to 2 colds per year; has had sinus pain previously but has never been treated for a sinus infection; no ear infections since childhood; regular dental care; reports persistent rhinorrhea of clear to yellow discharge, intermittent sneezing, and headache
Cardiovascular: Denies chest pain, palpitations
Respiratory: Only occasional nonproductive cough with this cold; no hemoptysis, no shortness of breath, no history of asthma
Gastrointestinal: No heartburn, nausea or vomiting, diarrhea, constipation
Female Reproductive: Uses IUD, light periods, erratic
Musculoskeletal: Denies myalgia, joint pain

Physical Examination

Vital signs: Temperature 98.6° F; pulse 72 bpm; respirations 16/min; BP 122/64 mm Hg; pulse oximetry 99% on room air
General: Well-groomed female, nontoxic in appearance and presenting without any acute distress
HEENT: No frontal or maxillary pain to palpitation and percussion; eyes watery; nasal mucosa swollen, red, no polyps; oral mucosa pink without lesions; pharynx slightly reddened, no purulent discharge noted; tonsils 2+; no pain elicited in ears; good light reflex in ear drums, landmarks visualized, no redness, retraction, or fluid noted; submandibular and submental nodes soft, slightly enlarged

Heart: S1, S2 with regular rate and rhythm; no murmurs, rubs, or gallops
Lungs: Clear to auscultation bilaterally
Abdomen: Soft, nontender to light palpation and nondistended; no hepatospleno-
   megaly; bowel sounds normoactive

After reviewing the case and the Grading Criteria in Appendix A, jot down your notes or preliminary answers in the spaces provided below. When you are ready to submit your answers for grading (if you are working with an instructor) and reflective feedback to help you evaluate your answers, go to **http://www.evolve.elsevier.com/Cappiello/** to complete this case.

Learning Issues

Before identifying your recommended Assessment and Plan, identify any learning issues that you believe are important for you to explore about this case:

Assessment

Please indicate the problems or issues you have identified that will guide your care (preferably in list form):

Continued

Plan

Please list your plans for addressing each of the problems or issues in your assessment:

Case 13

Jane Lincoln
Age 88 years

Opening Scenario

The medical assistant tells you that a nursing home called to let you know that Ms. Lincoln's purified protein derivative (PPD) test was negative. Ms. Lincoln is the patient of one of your associates who will be away for the next week and for whom you are covering. She was just admitted to the nursing home 3 days ago.

After reviewing the case and the Grading Criteria in Appendix A, jot down your notes or preliminary answers in the spaces provided below. When you are ready to submit your answers for grading (if you are working with an instructor) and reflective feedback to help you evaluate your answers, go to http://www.evolve.elsevier.com/Cappiello/ to complete this case.

Learning Issues

Before identifying your recommended Assessment and Plan, identify any learning issues that you believe are important for you to explore about this case:

Continued

Assessment

Please indicate the problems or issues you have identified that will guide your care (preferably in list form):

Plan

Please list your plans for addressing each of the problems or issues in your assessment:

Case 14

Jake Marland
Age 8½ months

Opening Scenario

Jake Marland is an 8½-month-old male infant on your schedule for an ear infection.

History of Present Illness

(Obtained from mother)
"Jake was awake a lot last night, and I think he's been pulling at his right ear. He has had three ear infections before and I know amoxicillin doesn't work for him. He had a cold about four days ago with a runny nose and a mild cough. I gave him acetaminophen for the cold and it seemed to get better. No one else at home is sick."

Medical History

Normal spontaneous vaginal delivery. Apgar scores were 9 and 9. Had three episodes of acute otitis media (AOM) at two months (amoxicillin), three months (azithromycin), and six months (treated with amoxicillin-clavulanate). Immunization record is shown in Table 14-1. Mild effusion at four-month WCC. Developmental milestones are all within normal limits on previous visits. Currently he is able to sit well and has started to push himself backward on the ground when he is on his stomach. Sleeps about 10 hours per night. Likes to fall asleep drinking a bottle but has been switched to water. Takes evening nap but often skips morning nap. Growth is indicated in Table 14-2.

Family Medical History

MGM: 51 years old (breast cancer diagnosed four years ago)
MGF: 54 years old (A&W)
PGM: 47 years old (A&W)
PGF: 46 years old (HTN)
Mother: 26 years old (A&W)
Father: 25 years old (A&W)
Brother: 3 years old (A&W)

TABLE 14-1	Immunization Record for Jake Marland			
Vaccine	**Age**	**Initials**	**Notes**	
Hep B #1	1 day	KN		
Hep B #2	2 mo	MDO		
Hep B #3	6 mo	MDO		
RV #1	2 mo	MDO		
RV #2	4 mo	MDO		
RV #3	6 mo	MDO		
DTaP #1	2 mo	MDO	Pentacel[†]	
DTaP #2	4 mo	MDO	Pentacel	
DTaP #3	6 mo	MDO	Pentacel	
DTaP #4				
DTap #5				
Hib #1	2 mo	MDO	Pentacel	
Hib #2	4 mo	MDO	Pentacel	
Hib #3	6 mo	MDO	Pentacel	
Hib #4				
PCV #1	2 mo	MDO		
PCV #2	4 mo	MDO		
PCV #3	6 mo	MDO		
PCV #4				
IPV #1	2 mo	MDO	Pentacel	
IPV #2	4 mo	MDO	Pentacel	
IPV #3	6 mo	MDO	Pentacel	
IPV #4				
Influenza				

Measure	Age	Result	Percentile
Length	Birth	19 in	25th
	2 mo	23 in	31st
	4 mo	24¾ in	29th
	6 mo	26¼ in	32nd
Weight	Birth	7 lb, 12 oz	49th
	2 mo	12 lb	38th
	4 mo	14 lb, 12 oz	34th
	6 mo	17 lb, 4 oz	36th
Head circumference	Birth	13¾ in	32nd
	2 mo	15¾ in	33rd
	4 mo	16½ in	29th
	6 mo	17¼ in	43rd

TABLE 14-2 Growth of Jake Marland

Social History

Lives with both parents and older brother (now three years old). Father works as a highway department employee. Mother works part-time at convenience store (four mornings per week). Jake attends the local day-care center when his mother is working. Jake was just approved for Medicaid. Father smokes one-half pack per day but is trying to quit and smokes primarily outside. Mother has never smoked.

Medications

None

Allergies

NKDA

Review of Systems

(Obtained from mother)

General: Good energy level, no recent fevers, more fussy over the last 24 hours

Integumentary: No itching or rashes

HEENT: No history of head injury; had about three upper respiratory infections [URIs] since birth and three previous episodes of AOM; responds to voice and other sounds; vocalizes; no allergy

Respiratory: Mother denies evidence of shortness of breath, wheezing, or cough

Cardiovascular: No shortness of breath or cyanosis with normal activity. No excessive bruising; no history of transfusions

Gastrointestinal: No vomiting, constipation, or watery stools; 2 to 3 yellow/brown soft stools per day

Genitourinary: No odor to urine, approximately 6 to 8 wet diapers per day; circumcised

Musculoskeletal: No sign of joint pain or swelling

Neurological: No seizures

Physical Examination

Vital signs: Temperature 99.8° F (tympanic); pulse 98 bpm; respirations 28/min

Weight: 19 lb, 8 oz (41st percentile); *length:* 27½ in (34th percentile)

General: Well nourished, well developed; in no acute distress; age-appropriate behavior

HEENT: Normocephalic without masses or lesions; pupils equal, round, and reactive to light; positive red reflex; moderate amount of clear discharge present in both eyes; no redness of conjunctiva; nares patent and noninjected; throat without redness or lesions; *right* tympanic membrane (TM) noninjected, mobile, crisp cone of light visualized; *left* TM with amber fluid effusion noted; TM nonmobile; very mild injection at periphery; cone of light diffuse

Neck: Supple without thyromegaly or adenopathy

Thorax: Clear to auscultation and percussion

Heart: Regular rate and rhythm; no murmurs, rubs, or gallops

Genitourinary: Descended testes, circumcised

Abdominal/gastrointestinal: No hepatosplenomegaly; abdomen soft, nontender; bowel sounds normoactive

Extremities: Range of motion functionally intact; no cyanosis, clubbing, or edema

Neurological: Positive Babinski reflex

Nutrition: Eats from all four food groups; using commercial baby food and soft and ground table foods; utilizes Women, Infants, and Children (WIC) services; current formula is Enfamil with Iron, 28 ounces per day

After reviewing the case and the Grading Criteria in Appendix A, jot down your notes or preliminary answers in the spaces provided below. When you are ready to submit your answers for grading (if you are working with an instructor) and reflective feedback to help you evaluate your answers, go to **http://www.evolve.elsevier.com/Cappiello/** to complete this case.

Learning Issues

Before identifying your recommended Assessment and Plan, identify any learning issues that you believe are important for you to explore about this case:

Assessment

Please indicate the problems or issues you have identified that will guide your care (preferably in list form):

Plan

Please list your plans for addressing each of the problems or issues in your assessment:

Case 15

Maurice Lamontagne
Age 64 years

Opening Scenario

Maurice Lamontagne is a 64-year-old man who has not had any primary care for several years. When he tried to give blood last week, he was told that he was anemic. He called the office and asked for an appointment because of this. The office staff asked if you wanted him to have any laboratory tests. You ordered a CBC, which is now available (Table 15-1).

TABLE 15-1	Laboratory Test Results for Maurice Lamontagne	
CBC	**Result**	**Normal Range**
WBC	8.2	4.5–10.8
RBC	3.85 L	4.20–5.40
Hgb	10.9 L	12.0–16.0
Hct	32.2 L	37.0–47.0
MCV	79.2 L	81.0–99.0
MCH	26.9 L	27.0–32.0
MCHC	33.4	32.0–36.0
RDW	16.4 H	11.0–16.0
Platelets	221	150–450
Segs	64	50–65
Lymphocytes	23 L	25–45
Monocytes	9	0–10
Eosinophils	4	0–4

History of Present Illness

"I've been a little more tired than usual, but I've been busy at work. I'm getting close to retirement, so I figured I was just slowing down a bit. Nothing else is unusual at all. I avoid doctors if I can. I feel pretty good, but I tire easily."

Medical History

Inguinal hernia repair 20 years ago
Last colonoscopy was seven years ago; he was told he did not need another "for 10 years"

Family Medical History

MGM: Deceased at age 80 years old (pancreatic cancer)
MGF: Deceased at age 77 years old (heart attack)
PGM: Deceased at age 60 years old ("women's problems")
PGF: Deceased at age 74 years old (stroke)
Mother: 87 years old (A&W)
Father: Deceased age 80 years old (heart attack)
Daughter: 39 years old (A&W)
One brother: 60 years old (alcoholism)
Four grandchildren: None with health problems

Social History

Married for 44 years. Works as a project foreman for landscaping portion of local nursery. Due for retirement soon. Smoking: One pack per day for 30 years. Alcohol: "A couple of beers in the evening."

Medications

Multivitamin: One daily

Allergies

NKDA

Review of Systems

General: Good energy level in the morning but tires easily; denies significant weight change, fevers, chills, or night sweats
Integumentary: No itching or rashes

HEENT: No history of head injury; no corrective lenses; denies eye pain, excessive tearing, blurring, or change in vision; no tinnitus or vertigo; denies frequent colds, hay fever, or sinus problems

Neck: No lumps, goiters, or pain

Respiratory: Denies shortness of breath, no paroxysmal nocturnal dyspnea

Cardiovascular: No chest pain; no shortness of breath with normal activity. No excessive bruising; no history of transfusions.

Gastrointestinal: No nausea, vomiting, constipation, or diarrhea; denies belching, bloating, and black or clay-colored stools; no bright red blood per rectum; weight stable past 10 years

Genitourinary: No dysuria; no difficulty starting stream; urine seems a little darker lately

Musculoskeletal: Mild joint pain with significant activity

Neurological: No headaches, seizures

Endocrine: No polyuria, polyphagia, polydipsia; temperature tolerances good

Physical Examination

Vital signs: Temperature 98.4° F; pulse 98 bpm; respirations 20/min; BP 112/70 mm Hg

Height: 5 ft 10 in; *Weight:* 172 lb; *BMI:* 24.7

General: Well nourished, well developed; in no acute distress; appears younger than stated age

HEENT: Normocephalic without masses or lesions; pupils equal, round, and reactive to light; extraocular movements intact; sclera white, skin and conjunctiva are slightly pale; fundi benign; nares patent and noninjected; throat without redness or lesions

Neck: Supple without thyromegaly or adenopathy

Thorax: Clear to auscultation and percussion

Heart: Regular rate and rhythm; no murmurs, rubs, or gallops

Abdominal/gastrointestinal: No hepatosplenomegaly; abdomen soft, nontender; bowel sounds normoactive

Genitourinary: Normal male, circumcised, testicles without masses or tenderness

Rectal: No masses; prostate smooth and not enlarged; stool is brown and guaiac negative

Extremities: Range of motion functionally intact; no cyanosis, clubbing, or edema

Neurological: Reflexes 2+ at Achilles, patellar, biceps, triceps, and brachioradialis; no Babinski signs present

After reviewing the case and the Grading Criteria in Appendix A, jot down your notes or preliminary answers in the spaces provided below. When you are ready to submit your answers for grading (if you are working with an instructor) and reflective feedback to help you evaluate your answers, go to http://www.evolve.elsevier.com/Cappiello/ to complete this case.

Learning Issues

Before identifying your recommended Assessment and Plan, identify any learning issues that you believe are important for you to explore about this case:

Assessment

Please indicate the problems or issues you have identified that will guide your care (preferably in list form):

Plan

Please list your plans for addressing each of the problems or issues in your assessment:

1:30 PM

Jerome Wilson
Age 47 years

Opening Scenario

Jerome Wilson is a 47-year-old man on your schedule for a follow-up visit. He had an annual examination six months ago with elevated lipid levels. At that time, you recommended that he start lipid-lowering medication. Rather than using medication, Mr. Wilson preferred to try to improve his lipids by working on lifestyle changes for six months. He was started on a heart-healthy diet and an exercise and stress management plan. The results of his lipid profile drawn six months ago, as well as other tests ordered, are shown in Table 16-1 and Table 16-2.

Notes of Jerome Wilson's Visit Six Months Ago

Reason for Visit

Jerome Wilson is a 47-year-old man scheduled for a complete physical examination. It has been three years since his last physical with you.

History of Present Illness

"I am planning to increase my exercise level by joining a local fitness club. I thought it would be a good idea to schedule a physical before doing this. I feel fine and have not had any change in my health."

Medical History

No hospitalizations or surgery. Seen twice in the past for bursitis of the left shoulder, which required steroid injections. No hypertension, coronary artery disease (CAD), or diabetes mellitus.

Family Medical History

Mother: 71 years old (hypercholesterolemia, surgery at age 65 for vascular occlusion in the leg)

Father: 71 years old (Alzheimer's disease for three years)
Sister: 47 years old (current diagnosis of breast cancer)
Grandparents: All died many years ago; he does not know causes of death

Social History

Lives with wife and three children, ages 3, 8, and 12. Works as a certified public accountant in a large accounting firm. Nonsmoker for 15 years. Four drinks of alcohol per week. Three cups of coffee per day. Golfs two to three times a week in good weather.

Medications

None

Allergies

NKDA

Review of Systems

General: States energy level is good; sleeps well; feels healthy but stressed keeping up with family and work responsibilities
Integumentary: Dry, itchy areas on scalp
HEENT: Denies problems with hearing; recently began to use reading glasses; sees dentist regularly
Respiratory: Denies any chest pain, shortness of breath, cough, or dyspnea on exertion
Gastrointestinal: No heartburn, nausea, abdominal pain; occasional constipation with occasional painful hemorrhoid; no rectal bleeding
Genitourinary: No dysuria, frequency, hesitancy, nocturia
Musculoskeletal: No current joint pain, but occasionally (every few months) notes transient joint pain in knees, wrists, and fingers; uses aspirin or acetaminophen when needed with good relief of symptoms
Neurological: No headaches; denies depression, memory changes

Physical Examination

Vital signs: Temperature 98.0° F; pulse 72 bpm; respirations 16/min; BP 136/74 mm Hg
Height: 5 ft 8 in; *weight:* 160 lb; *BMI:* 24
General: Healthy-appearing male who appears his stated age
Skin: Dry, scaly patches (approximately six areas ranging ½–1 cm in size on scalp); no other lesions

HEENT: Pupils equal and reactive to light, extraocular movements intact, fundi benign; nares patent and noninjected; throat without redness or lesions

Neck: Supple without thyromegaly or adenopathy

Heart: Regular rate and rhythm; no murmurs, rubs, or gallops

Lungs: Clear to auscultation

Abdominal/gastrointestinal: Abdomen soft, nontender, without hepatosplenomegaly; bowel sounds normoactive; digital rectal examination without masses; stools negative for occult blood

Genitourinary: No lesions or discharge noted; no testicular masses; no hernias noted; prostate firm, no nodules or enlargement

Extremities: Range of motion functionally intact; no redness, pain, or swelling noted; no edema, cyanosis, clubbing

Neurological: Reflexes 2+ at Achilles, patellar, biceps, triceps, brachioradialis; no Babinski signs

Assessment

- Hyperlipidemia
- Seborrheic dermatitis
- Recurrent joint pain
- Constipation with recurring hemorrhoid
- S/P bursitis left shoulder
- Family history of hypercholesterolemia

Plan

- Health coaching for healthy lifestyle changes. Assessed readiness to make changes in dietary, exercise, and stress management behaviors. Patient's plan and short-term goals:
  - Healthy eating: Dietary plan that reduces saturated fat and emphasizes fruits, vegetables, whole grains, low-fat dairy products, poultry, fish, and nuts. Limit red meat and sugary foods and beverages. Dietitian referral.
  - Increase exercise: Plans to incorporate 30 minutes of moderate-intensity exercise per day, five days per week (swimming, walking, biking). Instructed on how to check pulse and calculate target heart rate zone. To schedule appointment with fitness trainer at gym for muscle strengthening program with slow, gentle progression to avoid joint pain. To choose fitness app to track workouts.
  - Reduce stress: Plans to incorporate 5 to 10 minutes of meditation after work during the week. Directed to website for free guided mindfulness meditation podcasts.
- Ketoconazole-containing over-the-counter dandruff shampoo for seborrheic dermatitis.
- Increase fiber and water in diet for constipation.
- Hepatitis C as routine screening because he has not been tested.
- Return in six months for fasting lipid profile and review of lifestyle changes.

TABLE 16-1 Laboratory Test Results for Jerome Wilson from 6 Months Ago

Chemistry Profile

Test	Result	Normal Range
Calcium	9.0	8.4–10.2 mg/dL
Phosphorus	4.4	2.7–4.5 mg/dL
Glucose	90	70–105 mg/dL
BUN	21	6–26 mg/dL
Creatinine	1.4	0.7–1.6 mg/dL
BUN/creatinine	15	6–35
Uric acid	5.5	3.4–7.0 mg/dL
Cholesterol	281	150–200 mg/dL
Triglycerides	205	50–175 mg/dL
Total protein	7.7	6.9–8.2 g/dL
Albumin	4.4	3.4–5.3 g/dL
Globulin	3.3	2.0–4.0 g/dL
A/G ratio	1.3	1.0–2.2
ALP	89	39–117 U/L
LDH	192	118–273 U/L
AST (SGOT)	18	0–37 U/L
ALT (SGPT)	23	0–40 U/L
Total bilirubin	0.5	0–1.0 mg/dL

Urinalysis

Test	Result
Appearance	Clear
Color	Yellow
SG	1.010
pH	5.5
Protein	Negative
Glucose	Negative
Ketones	Negative
Blood	Negative

TABLE 16-1	Laboratory Test Results for Jerome Wilson from 6 Months Ago—Cont'd
Nitrite	Negative
Bilirubin	Negative
Leukocytes	Negative
Hepatitis C antibody	negative

Fasting lipid profile

Test	Result	Normal Range
Cholesterol	257	<200 mg/dL
Triglycerides	174	50–175 mg/dL
High-density lipoprotein cholesterol (HDL-C)	38	35–96 mg/dL
Low-density lipoprotein cholesterol (LDL-C)	204	0–190 mg/mL

TABLE 16-2	Risk Level at Which CVD Events Prevented (Benefit) Exceeds GI Harms			
	MEN 10-year CHD risk		WOMEN 10-year stroke risk	
Age 45–59 years	≥4%	Age 55–59 years	≥3%
Age 60–69 years	≥9%	Age 60–69 years	≥8%
Age 70–79 years	≥12%	Age 70–79 years	≥11%

This table applies to adults who are not taking nonsteroidal antiinflammatory drugs (NSAIDs) and who do not have upper gastrointestinal (GI) pain or a history of GI ulcers (U.S. Preventive Services Task Force, 2009a).

Today's Visit

Reason for Visit

Follow-up of lipid screening (Box 16-1).

History of Present Illness

Works out at a health club three days a week, swims three days a week, and does muscle strengthening program with machines twice a week. Remains a nonsmoker and has two to three drinks of alcohol per week. Continues to work in a high-pressure job.

BOX 16-1	Lipid Profile for Jerome Wilson of 3 Days Ago		
Test		**Result**	**Normal Range**
Cholesterol		221	>200 mg/dL
Triglycerides		157	50–175 mg/dL
High-density lipoprotein cholesterol (HDL-C)		38	35–96 mg/dL
Low-density lipoprotein cholesterol (LDL-C)		152	0–190 mg/mL

Review of Systems

General: States he met with the dietitian for two visits; he spoke with her right after the visit of 6 months ago and then 1 month later; he feels he has changed his diet significantly but has difficulty making wise choices when eating out

Integumentary: Scalp problem improved with ketoconazole shampoo; no longer needs to use shampoo

Cardiovascular: Denies chest pain

Respiratory: Denies shortness of breath, cough, dyspnea on exertion

Gastrointestinal: Continues to have occasional constipation with occasional flare-up of his hemorrhoid

Musculoskeletal: No recent joint pain; thinks his program of muscle strengthening at the gym may be helping this

Physical Examination

Vital signs: Temperature 97.6° F; pulse 70 bpm; respirations 16/min; BP 130/70 mm Hg

BMI: 24

Skin: No patches on scalp

Heart: Regular rate and rhythm; no murmurs, rubs, or gallops

Lungs: Clear to auscultation

After reviewing the case and the Grading Criteria in Appendix A, jot down your notes or preliminary answers in the spaces provided below. When you are ready to submit your answers for grading (if you are working with an instructor) and reflective feedback to help you evaluate your answers, go to **http://www.evolve.elsevier.com/Cappiello/** to complete this case.

Learning Issues

Before identifying your recommended Assessment and Plan, identify any learning issues that you believe are important for you to explore about this case:

Assessment

Please indicate the problems or issues you have identified that will guide your care (preferably in list form):

Plan

Please list your plans for addressing each of the problems or issues in your assessment:

1:45 PM

Dolores Sanchez
Age 16 years

Opening Scenario

Dolores Sanchez is a 16-year-old female scheduled for a contraceptive visit.

History of Present Illness

"I want to discuss birth control today. I have a boyfriend and have been using condoms for a while, but I want something more effective. Some of my friends use the shot and have gained weight. Will the pill make me gain weight?"
Dolores states that she has been having intercourse on an infrequent basis over the past year. Now she has a steady partner and is having intercourse approximately twice a week for the past two months. Dolores states that she is currently having a regular, normal period that started three days ago.

Dolores goes on to say that although she has heard about birth control methods such as the implant and IUDs, her older sister uses the pill and likes the pill as a method. Dolores assumes that she, too, will do well with the pill.

Medical History

No hospitalizations, surgeries, or major medical problems. She has had all of the usual childhood immunizations: MMR, Hepatitis B, IPV, varicella, HIBPCV13, DTaP series as a child, and diphtheria and Tdap as a booster at age 11. She started the HPV series with the first dose given one year ago. She did not return for subsequent doses.

Family Medical History

MGM: 72 years old (breast cancer, treated with radiation)
MGF: 73 years old (lung problems, smoker)
PGM: 70 years old (hypercholesterolemia)
PGF: Deceased at age 69 years old (MI)
Mother: 40 years old (asthmatic, smoker)

Father: 42 years old (HTN, hypercholesterolemia)
Siblings: Two brothers, 14 years old and 12 years old; sister, 18 years old (all healthy)

Social History

Smokes one-half pack per day. She had her first cigarette at age 13. Had smoked infrequently until last year when she began to smoke regularly with her friends. Is a sophomore in high school; enjoys school and maintains a B grade average. Is not involved in school sports other than physical education class twice a week. On yearbook committee. Lives at home with both parents. Works part-time in a convenience store. Denies drug use; occasional beer with friends. CAGE questions: Negative responses. Uses seatbelts. Denies history of intimate partner violence.

Medications

Occasional ibuprofen 400 mg for menstrual cramps

Allergies

NKDA

Review of Systems

General: Alert, healthy-appearing young female
HEENT: Ear infections as a child but not since age 10; denies asthma, hay fever, frequent colds, nasal discharge, sinus problems; no dental problems, but does not have regular preventive dental care
Cardiovascular: No history of heart murmur or heart problems
Respiratory: Denies any difficulty with breathing, asthma, or bronchitis
Abdominal/gastrointestinal: Denies heartburn, abdominal pain, constipation, diarrhea, rectal bleeding; no history of liver or gallbladder disease
Genitourinary: Menarche, age 12; menses, regular 28- to 30-day cycles, lasting 5 days; describes flow as moderate for 3 days, lighter for 2 days; experiences cramping on day 1 of cycle for which she uses ibuprofen 400 mg 2 to 3 times a day for 1 day with relief of cramping; denies intermenstrual or postcoital bleeding or dyspareunia; first intercourse at age 15½; two sexual partners, infrequent intercourse until 2 months ago; no complaints of vaginal discharge, itching, burning, or urinary dysuria or frequency; LMP started 1 week ago, normal menses, has not had intercourse since LMP; is planning on becoming more sexually active with current partner
Neurological: Headache on first day of menses that is relieved by the ibuprofen; no other complaints of headaches, no history of migraines; no history of seizures

Endocrine: States she is fatigued on the three days a week that she works after school because she must stay up late to finish homework; is not fatigued if she has 8 hours of sleep at night; no history of diabetes

Musculoskeletal: No complaint; no history of injuries, muscle pain, or joint pain

Physical Examination

Vital signs: Temperature 98.2° F; BP 120/62 mm Hg

Height: 5 ft 6 in; *weight:* 160 lb; *BMI:* 25.8

After reviewing the case and the Grading Criteria in Appendix A, jot down your notes or preliminary answers in the spaces provided below. When you are ready to submit your answers for grading (if you are working with an instructor) and reflective feedback to help you evaluate your answers, go to **http://www.evolve.elsevier.com/Cappiello/** to complete this case.

Learning Issues

Before identifying your recommended Assessment and Plan, identify any learning issues that you believe are important for you to explore about this case:

Assessment

Please indicate the problems or issues you have identified that will guide your care (preferably in list form):

Continued

Plan

Please list your plans for addressing each of the problems or issues in your assessment:

2:00 PM

Maria O'Malley
Age 13 years

Opening Scenario

Maria O'Malley is a 13-year-old female who has been seen previously in your practice. She comes today accompanied by her mother for evaluation of right ankle pain, which has bothered her for the past two weeks.

History of Present Illness

"My right ankle has been bothering me for two weeks. I don't remember any specific event that caused the ankle to begin hurting. It only hurts when I'm playing soccer, running and jumping, and kicking the ball. It also hurts when I am ice skating with my precision skating team. It hurts while I am playing sports, but the pain goes away as soon as I finish practice. It doesn't hurt when I'm at home, just when I am playing sports, so I tend to forget about it when I get home. When I remembered to tell my mom, she tried to get me to take Aleve and put ice on it, but I didn't do that very often." Maria denies any swelling and describes the pain as dull and nonradiating, a 4 to 5 on a scale of 1 to 10 when the ankle is bothering her. She denies previous injury.

Medical History

A review of her past visits shows that she has been followed for routine care only. She is up to date on all immunizations. Most recent physical examination was six months ago. Menarche one year ago. Has denied any need for contraception. No surgeries or hospitalizations. Last menstrual period was one week ago.

Family Medical History

Mother: 45 years old (A&W)
Father: 50 years old (HTN and arthritis)
Siblings: Two brothers, 9 and 17 years old (A&W)

Social History

Eighth-grade student who lives with both parents and two brothers. Honor roll student. Nonsmoker. States no alcohol or drug use.

Medications

Occasional naproxen

Allergies

NKDA

Review of Systems

General: Alert, healthy appearing young female
Cardiovascular: No history of heart murmur or heart problems
Respiratory: Denies any difficulty with breathing, asthma, or bronchitis
Gastrointestinal: Denies heartburn, abdominal pain, constipation, diarrhea, rectal bleeding

Physical Examination

Vital signs: Temperature 98.2° F; pulse 88 bpm; respirations 20/min; BP 102/50 mm Hg
Height: 5 ft 6 in; *weight:* 125 lb *BMI:*21
General: Young adolescent female who appears healthy; in no acute distress
Musculoskeletal: Right ankle: No swelling, redness, ecchymosis; pain localized over the right distal tibial-fibula joint with some radiation proximally and distally into the midfoot with activity; tenderness palpated over the anterior tibiofibular ligament, made worse with internal and external rotation of the foot; nontender over the anterior talofibular, calcaneofibular, and posterior talofibular ligaments; Achilles tendon is nontender; no proximal fibula tenderness; tender to resisted peroneal stress; ankle range of motion is limited only in dorsiflexion; sensory and motor examinations intact distally. Left ankle: No swelling, redness; full range of motion; no tenderness noted
Extremities: No prior history of fractures or injuries, muscle pain, or joint pain.

After reviewing the case and the Grading Criteria in Appendix A, jot down your notes or preliminary answers in the spaces provided below. When you are ready to submit your answers for grading (if you are working with an instructor) and reflective feedback to help you evaluate your answers, go to **http://www.evolve.elsevier.com/Cappiello/** to complete this case.

Learning Issues

Before identifying your recommended Assessment and Plan, identify any learning issues that you believe are important for you to explore about this case:

Assessment

Please indicate the problems or issues you have identified that will guide your care (preferably in list form):

Plan

Please list your plans for addressing each of the problems or issues in your assessment:

Case 19

2:15 PM

Liang Wang
Age 13½ years

Opening Scenario

Liang Wang is a 13½-year-old female scheduled for a follow-up acne visit. Her facial blemishes have not gotten better, and she is requesting a dermatology referral.

History of Present Illness

"I was here about a month ago for a camp physical. I was started on erythromycin 2% topical twice a day after cleansing with benzoyl peroxide 5%. I didn't feel that I was having any results after three weeks, so I tried some Cleocin T that had been prescribed for one of my friends. Cleocin T was only slightly more effective than erythromycin. I do not want another topical; another friend of mine had a pill and that worked much better. I have been avoiding chocolate because my mother told me I should, and that seems to have helped a little." Her blemishes do not change related to menses. She has a few areas of acne on her back, but it is mostly on her face and chin.

Medical History

No hospitalizations or accidents. Immunizations up to date, including Tdap and HPV.

Family Medical History

MGM: DM, onset at about 60 years old
Mother: 33 years old (A&W)
Father: 34 years old (A&W)
MGF, PGF, PGM: A&W

Social History

High school student. Plays soccer. Academically strong. Attends dances. Denies current sexual activity. Denies any alcohol use. Is a nonsmoker.

Medications

Erythromycin and Cleocin T as described under HPI

Allergies

NKDA

Review of Systems

General: Denies fatigue, night sweats, no change in weight

HEENT: Denies diplopia, blurring, hearing impairment, sore throats, headaches; dental examination three months ago

Cardiovascular: Denies chest pain, palpitations, exercise intolerance. Denies excessive bruising.

Respiratory: Denies shortness of breath, dyspnea on exertion

Gastrointestinal: Denies anorexia, nausea, vomiting, constipation, diarrhea, black or clay-colored stools

Genitourinary: Notes that her periods are somewhat irregular with alternating every 28 days and the next about every 42 days, 5-day duration; denies heavy bleeding; menarche at age 11; denies dysuria, hematuria

Musculoskeletal: Denies joint or back pain, no trauma

Physical Examination

Camp Physical Examination for Liang Wang from One Month Ago

General: Appears stated age and healthy; skin of face has a moderate distribution of comedones and a few cysts; back comedones are also present

Vital signs: Temperature 97.4° F; pulse 66 bpm; respirations 16/min; BP 90/38 mm Hg

Height: 5 ft 1 in; *weight:* 97 lb; *BMI:* 18.3

HEENT: Head is normocephalic, atraumatic; pupils equal, round, and reactive to light; extraocular movements intact; tympanic membranes are observable without excessive cerumen; nares are patent without redness or exudate; throat is not injected, tongue is midline; palate rises symmetrically; teeth are in adequate repair; multiple facial comedones, a few of which are cystic

Neck: Supple without thyromegaly, adenopathy, or carotid bruits

Heart: Regular rate and rhythm; no murmurs, rubs, or gallops

Lungs: Clear to auscultation and percussion

Breasts: Examination is deferred related to age and indications

Back and chest: A few comedones

Abdominal: Soft, nontender; no hepatosplenomegaly

Extremities: No cyanosis, clubbing, or edema

Neurological: Reflexes are 2+ at the biceps, triceps, brachioradialis, patellar, and Achilles; no Babinski signs present; strength and sensation are symmetrical

---

After reviewing the case and the Grading Criteria in Appendix A, jot down your notes or preliminary answers in the spaces provided below. When you are ready to submit your answers for grading (if you are working with an instructor) and reflective feedback to help you evaluate your answers, go to **http://www.evolve.elsevier.com/Cappiello/** to complete this case.

Learning Issues

Before identifying your recommended Assessment and Plan, identify any learning issues that you believe are important for you to explore about this case:

Assessment

Please indicate the problems or issues you have identified that will guide your care (preferably in list form):

Plan

Please list your plans for addressing each of the problems or issues in your assessment:

Tess Ireland
45 years

Opening Scenario

Tess Ireland is a 45-year-old female on your schedule with a complaint of heartburn. She has been followed in your practice for several years. Her last physical examination was nine months ago. Her most recent visit was 2½ weeks ago for elbow pain.

History of Present Illness

"I've had severe heartburn for 10 to 12 days. I saw you 2½ weeks ago (see note) when I had a left elbow problem and you prescribed some medication for 10 days. During the last few days of treatment I began to develop severe heartburn, pain in my lower chest, and a feeling of stomach acid coming into my throat. I assumed this was due to the medication. I stopped drinking coffee (reluctantly) and tea and began to take Maalox. This helped, but the symptoms have not yet resolved even though I have finished the medication."

Note from 2½ Weeks Ago

Reason for Visit

This 45-year-old female known to your practice presents with a 10-day history of medial left elbow pain with some radiation down into the ring and little fingers. She has tried naproxen 220 mg (2 tablets twice a day) for the past week without significant improvement. She aggravated the elbow pain this past weekend by skiing and driving a long distance in her car. She had a similar bout six months ago, which was resolved with ice and OTC NSAIDs.

Medical History

Healthy individual. Physical examination and gynecological examination nine months ago. No surgeries or major illnesses.

Family Medical History

Mother: 77 years old (Parkinson's disease)
Father: Died at age 54 (myocardial infarction [MI])
Three paternal uncles with heart disease
Sister: 52 years old (A&W)
Siblings: Three brothers ages 45, 48, and 50; 50-year-old brother had MI at age 34 but is now doing well

Medications

Daily multivitamin

Allergies

NKDA

Review of Systems

General: No weight loss or gain, fatigue, or fever
HEENT: No complaints of eye, ear nose or dental pain, no headaches.
Respiratory: No complaints of shortness of breath; denies history of asthma, frequent respiratory infections, pneumonia or flu; denies wheezing, shortness of breath or dyspnea on exertion; cough is worse at night and improves with elevating head of bed.
Cardiovascular: Denies chest pain or discomfort, orthopnea, or paroxysmal nocturnal dyspnea
Gastrointestinal: No nausea, vomiting, lower abdominal pain, diarrhea, constipation, or blood in stools
Genitourinary: Regular menses; last menstrual period (LMP) three weeks ago; IUD for birth control

Physical Examination

There is no erythema, ecchymosis, atrophy, or deformity in the left upper extremity. She has a positive Tinel's sign over the ulnar nerve of the left elbow. No weakness noted. Left elbow, forearm: no erythema, ecchymosis, atrophy, or deformity. No pain with range of motion or palpation. Right arm: no significant findings.

Assessment

- Ulnar neuritis

Plan

- Avoid local pressure.
- Nabumetone 500 mg. po BID
- Return for follow-up if symptoms persist.

. . . .

Review of Systems

General: Denies recent weight loss or gain, fatigue or fever

HEENT: Denies problems with cold or flu; complains of frequent throat clearing; denies dysphagia, dysphonia or odynophagia; nonsmoker; no known environmental toxin exposure; denies eye, ear nose or dental pain

Respiratory: Complains of non-productive cough for 5 days; denies history of asthma, frequent respiratory infections, pneumonia, or flu; denies wheezing, shortness of breath or dyspnea on exertion; cough is worse at night and improves with elevating head of bed.

Cardiovascular: Denies chest pain or discomfort, orthopnea or paroxysmal nocturnal dyspnea

Gastrointestinal: Appetite good, low fat diet; complains of epigastric discomfort; denies difficulty swallowing, nausea, vomiting, lower abdominal pain, diarrhea, constipation, or blood in stools

Genitourinary: Regular menses, LMP 3 weeks ago; IUD for birth control

Musculoskeletal: Neuritis of left elbow "about 75% improved"; continues to ice area approximately once a day and is riding bicycle less; noticing other things that bother her elbow (carrying heavy objects in left arm and driving car); tries not to rest elbow on armrest of car door; if she has to use pressure with her left hand on the steering wheel, it bothers her elbow

Neurological: Denies paresthesia in left hand

Physical Examination

Vital signs: Temperature 98.0° F; pulse 68 beats/min; respirations 16/min; BP 130/68 mm Hg

Height: 5 ft 6 in; *weight:* 140 lb; *BMI:* 22.6

General: Healthy-appearing female

HEENT: No frontal or maxillary tenderness; nasal mucosa: red, clear exudate; tympanic membranes: crisp cone of light, landmarks visible; pharynx: noninjected, no exudates or lesions, uvula midline

Neck: Supple without thyromegaly, lymphadenopathy

Heart: Regular rate and rhythm, S1 and S2 normal; no murmurs, rubs, or gallops

Lungs: Clear to auscultation

Abdomen: Soft, nontender, nondistended, bowel sounds normoactive; no hepato-splenomegaly; no guarding, rigidity, or rebound

Extremities: No erythema, atrophy, deformity noted in upper extremities; Tinel's sign remains slightly positive over ulnar nerve in left elbow; no lower extremity edema

Neurological: Sensory function intact bilaterally to light touch in upper extremities

After reviewing the case and the Grading Criteria in Appendix A, jot down your notes or preliminary answers in the spaces provided below. When you are ready to submit your answers for grading (if you are working with an instructor) and reflective feedback to help you evaluate your answers, go to **http://www.evolve.elsevier.com/Cappiello/** to complete this case.

Learning Issues

Before identifying your recommended Assessment and Plan, identify any learning issues that you believe are important for you to explore about this case:

Assessment

Please indicate the problems or issues you have identified that will guide your care (preferably in list form):

Plan

Please list your plans for addressing each of the problems or issues in your assessment:

Case 21

3:15 PM

Michael Smith
Age 24 years

. . . .

Opening Scenario

Michael Smith is a 24-year-old male scheduled for a complete physical examination. This is his first visit in your office.

History of Present Illness

"I have intermittent episodes of diarrhea, abdominal discomfort and cramps, bloating, and—on occasion—constipation. Often when I am eating, or right after I finish, I need to run to the bathroom and I have diarrhea and cramps. The cramps are gone after I have a bowel movement. Later I have gas and bloating. I hate mornings. I feel sick every morning. I'm bloated, nauseous, and can have a few watery stools before I can get out of the house. I need to know where every bathroom is when away from home. The cramping and gas can be excruciating, and I have missed activities because of this. This is difficult because currently I'm in a class that requires an outdoor experience. I'm expected to spend time doing research in the mountains, which means day hikes without a nearby bathroom. It's a nightmare. I would do overnight camping trips in this program if this were not such a problem. I don't know what size clothes to buy because I need a larger size for the days I have a lot of bloating, but if I have a few good days, then I wear a size smaller."

The patient feels as if he is not evacuating his bowels completely, giving him the sensation of constipation. He has three to five loose to semiformed stools per day. Stools are often urgent. Rarely, he has mucus in his stools; there is no blood in stools. Symptoms are almost daily. The only thing that helps the cramping is to lie down. He does not waken at night to have a bowel movement, but he states that first thing in the morning, he is "running to the bathroom."

He was seen elsewhere for this problem one year ago. At that time he was diagnosed with possible *Giardia*. His stool cultures were negative, but the diagnosis was made presumptively based on his history of extensive world travel. He was treated with a trial of metronidazole and did not improve. He did not follow up with that provider.

Symptoms have been present since at least his freshman year in high school. He has tried Imodium and Pepto-Bismol occasionally with limited results. He occasionally has no stool for a day or two, especially after taking Imodium. He occasionally has a "normal" stool. He denies laxative use.

Medical History

No hospitalizations or surgery. Up-to-date on all childhood immunizations, including tetanus 5 years ago and hepatitis B in high school. No hepatitis A immunization. Flu shot current. Past health concerns have been abdominal pain, bloating, and diarrhea. No history of gallbladder disease, diabetes, or cancer.

Family Medical History

MGM: 70 years old (A&W)
MGF: 71 years old (hypertension)
PGM: 66 years old (breast cancer)
PGF: 67 years old (arthritis)
Mother: 45 years old (A&W), has had "stomach problems"
Father: 47 years old (A&W)
Sister: 19 years old (A&W)
No family history of IBD, celiac disease, colon cancer, or polyps

Social History

Patient has a good relationship with his girlfriend. He sees parents frequently. They understand this problem. He is currently a graduate student with a stressful lifestyle. Previously, he worked on a cruise ship, which took him all over the world. His alcohol intake was high in the past as a college student, up to two to three six-packs of beer on the weekends, which gave him loose stools. Rarely has he used alcohol over the past two years. He denies intravenous or intranasal drug use or other recreational drug use and has never smoked cigarettes. His caffeine intake is one to two cups of coffee and one to two regular colas a day. Exercises intermittently.

Medications

None on a regular basis. Infrequent antibiotic use, thinking he had penicillin for a strep throat in high school and amoxicillin for sinusitis three years ago. Has occasional Imodium or Pepto-Bismol "when diarrhea is bad." No regular NSAID use, only occasional Advil for a headache, less than once a week.

Allergies

Had "hay fever as a child." NKDA

Review of Systems

General: Good appetite with no weight loss, but does not eat at times due to fear of diarrhea and pain; no fatigue; no fever, chills; no blood transfusions; sleeps 6 to 7 hours per night

Integumentary: No lesions or rashes

HEENT: Denies any vision problems, no glasses; sees dentist twice a year; no ear or hearing problems; no nasal discharge or bleeding; denies sore throat

Cardiovascular: No chest pain, palpitations

Respiratory: No shortness of breath, coughing, wheezing, or asthma

Gastrointestinal: Frequent nausea, no vomiting; heartburn two to three times a week

Genitourinary: Sex life affected slightly because sometimes he feels sick and just wants to "be still"; no dysuria or frequency; heterosexual; denies homosexual or bisexual contact

Musculoskeletal: No joint pain or swelling, arthritis, no muscle pain or swelling

Endocrine: No skin or hair changes; temperature tolerances good

Neurological: No weakness, seizures, numbness, or dizziness; occasional "stress" headache relieved by Advil; denies depression but states that sometimes this health problem "gets him down"

Physical Examination

Vital signs: Temperature 98.0° F; pulse 70 bpm; respirations 16/min; BP 120/80 mm Hg

Height: 5 ft 11 in; *weight:* 175 lb; *BMI:* 24

General: Well nourished, well developed

Skin: No rashes, lesions, scars

HEENT: Eyes: no redness or lesions; extraocular movements intact. Ear: no discharge; tympanic membrane intact, crisp cone of light. Nose: no exudate, polyps. Mouth: no lesions, good dentition

Neck: No lymphadenopathy or thyromegaly

Heart: Regular rate and rhythm; no murmurs, rubs, or gallops

Lungs: Clear to auscultation, no wheezes

Abdominal: Soft, no masses, no hepatosplenomegaly; slight, diffuse tenderness in lower abdomen. Rectal: external—no masses, lesions, irritation; internal—normal sphincter tone, no anal fissures or hemorrhoids; palpable, nontender; soft brown stool, heme negative; prostate firm, nontender

Genitourinary: Without palpable inguinal nodes; circumcised penis; without lesions, edema, erythema, masses of genitalia; testes palpated without masses, tenderness; negative bilaterally for direct inguinal hernias

Extremities: No edema; pedal pulses palpable bilaterally; warm, pink, good muscle strength bilaterally in upper and lower extremities, normal reflexes

Neurological: Alert, oriented ×3, speech, gait, and affect normal; cranial nerves 2 through 12 intact

Nutritional: Eats one to three meals a day depending on his activities; when life is more settled, such as on vacation, he eats regularly and makes better food choices; last night had a huge steak and potato with blue cheese dip, which caused diarrhea; for lunch had some corn chips, which caused cramps; for breakfast, had cereal and milk, which again caused bloating; denies milk is causing his problems; does not chew gum

After reviewing the case and the Grading Criteria in Appendix A, jot down your notes or preliminary answers in the spaces provided below. When you are ready to submit your answers for grading (if you are working with an instructor) and reflective feedback to help you evaluate your answers, go to **http://www.evolve.elsevier.com/Cappiello/** to complete this case.

Learning Issues

Before identifying your recommended Assessment and Plan, identify any learning issues that you believe are important for you to explore about this case:

Assessment

Please indicate the problems or issues you have identified that will guide your care (preferably in list form):

Plan

Please list your plans for addressing each of the problems or issues in your assessment:

4:00 PM

Timothy Gifford
Age 4 years

Opening Scenario

Timothy Gifford is a 4-year-old boy on your schedule for possible head lice. His family is present.

History of Present Illness

(Obtained from mother)
"Timmy has head lice. He got rid of them when I used some medication I had left over from one of my older kids who had lice, but the people next door didn't get their kids treated, so Timmy got them again. I need something for him and for all the rest of us too. If you could give us the stuff that doesn't require picking off the nits I'd appreciate it." Timmy and his mother deny any other irritated, open, or itching areas on his body.

Medical History

None

Medications

None

Allergies

NKDA

Review of Systems

(Obtained from mother)
General: Good energy level, eats well, sleeps well
Integumentary: No itching or rashes apart from head lice

HEENT: Denies frequent colds, seasonal allergies; teeth present without obvious caries, brushes teeth with parent assistance

Respiratory: Denies cough, wheezing; no snoring

Physical Examination

Vital signs: Temperature 97.2° F; pulse 88 bpm; respirations 22/min

Weight: 51 lb

HEENT: Small, white "balls" clinging to his hair shafts scattered all over his head; they are approximately $1/16$ in from the scalp; no lice are seen; his head is slightly red, and there are three to four open areas of scratching lesions without purulent drainage; no nits seen in eyelashes; no cervical adenopathy; conjunctiva are without redness or discharge

Neck: No lumps, goiters, or pain

Heart: Regular rate and rhythm

Respiratory: Clear to auscultation

Extremities: No lesions seen on arms and trunk

After reviewing the case and the Grading Criteria in Appendix A, jot down your notes or preliminary answers in the spaces provided below. When you are ready to submit your answers for grading (if you are working with an instructor) and reflective feedback to help you evaluate your answers, go to **http://www.evolve.elsevier.com/ Cappiello/** to complete this case.

Learning Issues

Before identifying your recommended Assessment and Plan, identify any learning issues that you believe are important for you to explore about this case:

Assessment

Please indicate the problems or issues you have identified that will guide your care (preferably in list form):

Plan

Please list your plans for addressing each of the problems or issues in your assessment:

Case 23

4:00 PM

Rita Davison
Age 54 years

Opening Scenario

Rita Davison is a 54-year-old female known to your practice for many years. She is on your schedule today for problems with blood sugar levels.

History of Present Illness

"My blood sugar levels have been higher. My usual blood sugar levels are in the 100 to 150 range, and I have had several over 200 in the past week or so." You review her home glucose monitoring chart (Table 23-1).

Medical History

You review her old chart and find that she has a 10-year history of type 2 DM controlled by a no-concentrated-sweets diet, and metformin 1000 mg bid and glipizide XL 2.5 mg po daily in the morning. She tells you that she has been taking ibuprofen 400 mg every four hours or so for the past three or four days because she was playing more tennis and her back was starting to ache. Other than that, her history has been unremarkable.

Social History

Divorced for many years. New relationship with man that she has been riding motorcycles with. Has had a Harley-Davidson motorcycle for many years. Works as an associate at a major retail chain, mostly as a cashier. Two children and six grandchildren—all close and she spends a lot of time with them. Has never smoked. Light beer "every now and then." Less than three beers per week.

Medications

Metformin 1000 mg po bid
Glipizide XL 2.5 mg po daily in morning

90

TABLE 23-1	Home Glucose Monitoring Chart for Rita Davison	
Day	**Time**	**Result**
8 days ago	7 AM	210
8 days ago	4 PM	267
7 days ago	7 AM	199
6 days ago	7 AM	202
6 days ago	12 noon	274
6 days ago	8 PM	188
5 days ago	4 PM	211
5 days ago	8 PM	289
4 days ago	7 AM	220
4 days ago	4 PM	145
3 days ago	12 noon	178
2 days ago	7 AM	183
2 days ago	4 PM	244
1 day ago	7 AM	197
1 day ago	4 PM	203
1 day ago	8 PM	184
This morning	7 AM	190

Ibuprofen 400 mg po every four hours prn (OTC 200 mg tablets, two every 4 hours), taken three to four times a day for the past two weeks

Allergies

NKDA

Review of Systems

Negative

Physical Examination

Vital signs: Temperature 98.6° F; pulse 84 bpm; respirations 24/min; BP 144/86 mm Hg
Height: 5 ft 5 in; *weight:* 152 lb; *BMI:* 25.3
Point-of-care laboratory test: HgbA1C: 7.3 (previously running in the 6.5 range)

   NOTE: This case does not give you the complete physical examination stats. It intends to focus on what you are thinking about before you do your physical examination. You may also want to consider what should be included in the physical examination of this woman.

After reviewing the case and the Grading Criteria in Appendix A, jot down your notes or preliminary answers in the spaces provided below. When you are ready to submit your answers for grading (if you are working with an instructor) and reflective feedback to help you evaluate your answers, go to **http://www.evolve.elsevier.com/Cappiello/** to complete this case.

Learning Issues

Before identifying your recommended Assessment and Plan, identify any learning issues that you believe are important for you to explore about this case:

Assessment

Please indicate the problems or issues you have identified that will guide your care (preferably in list form):

Plan

Please list your plans for addressing each of the problems or issues in your assessment:

Case 24

Jay Leeds
Age 13

Opening Scenario

Jay Leeds is a 13-year-old boy who presents today with a two-day history of progressive pain in his right hemi-scrotum.

History of Present Illness

Denies fever, dysuria, urinary frequency, or scrotal trauma. Denies sexual activity. No gross hematuria. He rates the pain as 6 on a scale of 1 to 10. He has mild nausea but no vomiting. He took acetaminophen for the pain with minimal relief. Pain is made somewhat worse by activity but is pretty constant.

Medical History

No major illnesses. Immunizations up to date.

Social History

Lives with both parents and younger (age 8) sister. Denies smoking, alcohol use, drug use.

Medications

No medications

Allergies

NKDA

Review of Systems

General: Denies fatigue, night sweats; no change in weight

Gastrointestinal: Denies anorexia, nausea, vomiting, constipation, diarrhea, black or clay-colored stools

Genitourinary: See History of Present Illness

Physical Examination

General: Appears stated age and healthy

Abdominal: No masses, tenderness; no hepatosplenomegaly, no flank tenderness, no bladder distention

Genitourinary: Darkened and swollen right testis, no obvious inguinal hernia, scrotum with no discrepancies in size or presence of erythema

After reviewing the case and the Grading Criteria in Appendix A, jot down your notes or preliminary answers in the spaces provided below. When you are ready to submit your answers for grading (if you are working with an instructor) and reflective feedback to help you evaluate your answers, go to **http://www.evolve.elsevier.com/ Cappiello/** to complete this case.

Learning Issues

Before identifying your recommended Assessment and Plan, identify any learning issues that you believe are important for you to explore about this case:

Assessment

Please indicate the problems or issues you have identified that will guide your care (preferably in list form):

Plan

Please list your plans for addressing each of the problems or issues in your assessment:

Case 25

Sharon Goldstein
Age 23 years

Opening Scenario

It is now the end of a busy day. Your desk has a stack of charts on it that require your attention. The chart of Sharon Goldstein has two laboratory reports attached to the front (Tables 25-1 and 25-2).

You review your note of last week on Ms. Goldstein. What is your plan for follow-up of this Pap smear report?

TABLE 25-1	Gynecological Cytology for Sharon Goldstein from 1 Week Ago

Gynecological History:

- LMP: 10 days ago
- Pregnant: No
- Postpartum: No
- Menopause: No
- Oral contraceptives: Yes
- IUD: No
- Other: None

Slides received: 1
Gynecological source: Ectocervical/endocervical smear
Statement of adequacy: Satisfactory; endocervical component present
Gynecological diagnosis: Atypical squamous cells of undetermined significance (ASCUS)
Additional comments: Inflammatory smear
Gynecological follow-up recommendation: Recommend repeat cytology
Ann Smith, MD

TABLE 25-2	Vaginal Swab for Sharon Goldstein from 1 Week Ago

Negative for *Chlamydia* and *Gonorrhea*

Note of Sharon Goldstein's Visit of Last Week

History of Present Illness

This 24-year-old single female presents for an office visit as she has developed spotting with her implant and she is due for her annual gynecological examination. She states that she is in good health. She is happy with her contraceptive choice. She has had regular, light menses with infrequent spotting since the implant was inserted 1.5 years ago. Last episode of spotting was 10 days ago, light, lasting 2 days. She denies headaches, chest pain, abdominal pain, eye changes, or shortness of breath. She has engaged in intercourse with her current boyfriend for 6 months. Used condoms in beginning of relationship for 1 month but no longer using protection.

Medical History

No history of surgery or major medical problems. Up-to-date on usual childhood immunizations. Only received one of the three HPV vaccines. Last tetanus immunization was 9 years ago.

Family Medical History

MGM: 68 years old (A&W)
MGF: 71 years old (HTN)
PGM: 64 years old (rheumatoid arthritis)
PGF: 70 years old (emphysema)
Mother: 43 years old (A&W)
Father: 49 years old (A&W)
Two sisters: 17, 19 years old (A&W)

Social History

Works in retail at the mall. Lives in apartment with roommates. Smokes 1 pack per day. Walks to work six blocks each workday and is on her feet all day. Likes to go to beach and swim on day off. Eats two meals per day. Drinks three diet colas per day. No coffee or tea. No milk; usually has cheese once a day. Vegetables are usually potatoes and a daily salad. Fruits are orange juice in the morning. Two to three beers about three times a week. Denies illicit drug use. Denies any concerns regarding domestic violence. Always uses seatbelts.

Medications

Nexplanon
Daily multivitamin

Allergies

Penicillin (rash)

Review of Systems

General: Feels very healthy; no complaints of fatigue
HEENT: Wears contacts; routine dental care; denies history of allergies, frequent colds, sore throats; no ear pain, hearing loss
Cardiovascular: No history of rheumatic fever, heart murmur, or chest pain
Respiratory: Denies shortness of breath, asthma, bronchitis
Gastrointestinal: No complaints of heartburn, stomach problems, diarrhea, constipation, or hemorrhoids
Genitourinary: Menarche at age 12; cycles (before using the implant) 27-day, regular, 4 to 5 days of moderate flow with mild cramping; no postcoital bleeding or dyspareunia; since implant use, her menses are regular but lighter, lasting 3 days; infrequent light spotting, occurring 1 to 2 days every 3 to 4 months; LMP 21 days ago; no complaints of vaginal discharge, itching, burning, or odor; no history of STIs; two previous sexual partners; history of one UTI 2 years ago; G0P0
Musculoskeletal: No history of fractures, sprains; no joint or muscle pain
Endocrine: Good energy level; temperature tolerances good
Neurological: Only occasional stress headache; no weakness, paresthesias, depression

Physical Examination

Vital signs: Temperature 98.0° F; pulse 88 bpm; respirations 18/min; BP 112/66 mm Hg
HEENT: No oral lesions; good dentition
Neck: No lymphadenopathy, thyromegaly
Heart: Regular rate and rhythm; no murmurs, rubs, or gallops
Lungs: Clear to auscultation
Abdominal: No masses, tenderness; no hepatosplenomegaly
Pelvic: Vulva: no redness, discharge, lesions. Vagina: no redness, discharge, lesions. Cervix: pink, no visible lesions. Uterus: small, smooth, firm, AV/AF. Adnexa: no enlargement or tenderness. Wet mount: negative

After reviewing the case and the Grading Criteria in Appendix A, jot down your notes or preliminary answers in the spaces provided below. When you are ready to submit your answers for grading (if you are working with an instructor) and reflective feedback to help you evaluate your answers, go to **http://www.evolve.elsevier.com/ Cappiello/** to complete this case.

Learning Issues

Before identifying your recommended Assessment and Plan, identify any learning issues that you believe are important for you to explore about this case:

Assessment

Please indicate the problems or issues you have identified that will guide your care (preferably in list form):

Plan

Please list your plans for addressing each of the problems or issues in your assessment:

Case 26

Phil Noonan

Age 38 years

Opening Scenario

The office staff tells you that Phil Noonan is on the phone, and he is really upset because he just "filled the toilet bowl with blood." They want to know whether you want to send him to the emergency room (ER) or talk to him on the phone.

Depending on your decision, refer to the appropriate section of the Case Discussion.

After reviewing the case and the Grading Criteria in Appendix A, jot down your notes or preliminary answers in the spaces provided below. When you are ready to submit your answers for grading (if you are working with an instructor) and reflective feedback to help you evaluate your answers, go to **http://www.evolve.elsevier.com/ Cappiello/** to complete this case.

Learning Issues

Before identifying your recommended Assessment and Plan, identify any learning issues that you believe are important for you to explore about this case:

Continued

Assessment

Please indicate the problems or issues you have identified that will guide your care (preferably in list form):

Plan

Please list your plans for addressing each of the problems or issues in your assessment:

Annie Littlefield
Age 2½ years

Opening Scenario

A phone call is received from the mother of a 2½-year-old girl known to your practice. Her mother is hysterical, stating that her daughter just passed what looked like a 12-inch-long strand of spaghetti in the toilet. She states that she knows food is not passed undigested and wonders what this could be. Is it a worm?

Medical History

A review of the records indicates that this child has been followed since birth in your office. There is no history of any major illnesses. Annie is up to date on all immunizations and has had all her routine checkups. Her last well-child check was three months ago with normal growth and development. About two months ago Annie spent time with her grandmother in a rural area of Georgia.

Medications

No medications—Annie is low risk for dental caries.

Allergies

NKDA

After reviewing the case and the Grading Criteria in Appendix A, jot down your notes or preliminary answers in the spaces provided below. When you are ready to submit your answers for grading (if you are working with an instructor) and reflective feedback to help you evaluate your answers, go to http://www.evolve.elsevier.com/Cappiello/ to complete this case.

Learning Issues

Before identifying your recommended Assessment and Plan, identify any learning issues that you believe are important for you to explore about this case:

Assessment

Please indicate the problems or issues you have identified that will guide your care (preferably in list form):

Plan

Please list your plans for addressing each of the problems or issues in your assessment:

DAY **TWO**

Case 28

8:00 AM

Kerry Bailey

Age 15 years

Opening Scenario

Kerry Bailey is a 15-year-old girl in your office for a sport physical. She went to soccer practice yesterday, and the coach told her that she could not come back until she had her forms filled out and signed.

History of Present Illness

"I have good exercise tolerance. I have no pain, shortness of breath, dizziness, or any other symptoms associated with exercise currently or in the past. Nothing has changed since last year, so why do I have to keep coming here?" Miss Bailey has no current illnesses. She is only here for a preparticipation physical evaluation (PPE).

Medical History

No hospitalizations, surgeries, or major illnesses. Immunization record is shown in Table 28-1.

Family Medical History

No history of diabetes mellitus or cardiac problems. No history of sudden death.

Social History

Miss Bailey is a student, and she is happy in school. Feels she is doing well (A-/B+ grade average). Plays soccer. Does not feel excessively stressed at home. Youngest of two children. Brother is in his first year of college. She denies alcohol or drug intake and sexual activity.

Medications

Multivitamin daily

TABLE 28-1	Immunization Record for Kerry Bailey, 15 years old							
Vaccine	Date	Initials	Notes		Vaccine	Date	Initials	Notes
Hep B #1	Birth				PCV7 #3	6 mo	SP	
Hep B #2	2 mo	MDO			PCV7 #4	15 mo	MDO	
Hep B #3	6 mo	SP			PCV13	15 mo	MDO	
RV #1	2 mo	MDO			IPV #1	2 mo	MDO	
RV #2	4 mo	KJ			IPV #2	4 mo	KJ	
RV #3	6 mo	SP			IPV #3	6 mo	SP	
DTaP #1	2 mo	MDO			IPV #4	4 yr	SA	
DTaP #2	4 mo	KJ			MMR #1	15 mo	MDO	
DTaP #3	6 mo	SP			MMR #2	4 yr	SA	
DTaP #4	18 mo	MDO			Varicella #1	15 mo	MDO	
DTaP #4	4 yr	SA			Varicella #2	4 yr	SA	
Tdap	12 yr	RR			Hep A #1	10 yr	SA	
Hib #1	2 mo	MDO			Hep A #2	11 yr	SA	
Hib #2	4 mo	KJ			HPV #1	12 yr		
Hib #3	6 mo	SP			HPV #2	12 yr 1 mo		
Hib #4	15 mo	MDO			HPV #3	12 yr 6 mo		
PCV7 #1	2 mo	MDO			MCV4	11 yr		
PCV7 #2	4 mo	KJ						

Allergies

NKDA

Review of Systems

General: Denies night sweats, swelling

HEENT: Denies diplopia, blurring, hearing impairment; no history of head injury, sore throats

Cardiovascular: Denies chest pain; no history of murmur, syncope. Denies hematuria and excessive bruising.

Respiratory: Denies shortness of breath, dyspnea on exertion, paroxysmal nocturnal dyspnea

Gastrointestinal: Denies anorexia, nausea, vomiting, constipation, diarrhea, black or clay-colored stools

Genitourinary: Denies dysuria

Musculoskeletal: Denies joint and back pain

Physical Examination

Vital signs: Temperature 98.2° F; pulse 82 bpm; respirations 20/min; BP 96/56 mm Hg

Height: 5 ft 6 in; *weight:* 133 lb

Skin: No lesions or rashes apparent

HEENT: Head is normocephalic, atraumatic; pupils equal, round, and reactive to light; extraocular movements intact; vision is 20/20 uncorrected; tympanic membranes are observable without excessive cerumen; nares are patent without redness or exudate; throat is noninjected; tongue is midline; palate rises symmetrically; teeth in adequate repair

Neck: Supple without thyromegaly, adenopathy, or carotid bruits

Heart: Regular rate and rhythm; no rubs or gallops; a grade II/VI distinctive vibratory early systolic murmur is heard at the third left ICS LSB with the patient in a sitting position; murmur is decreased with the patient supine. When Ms. Bailey changes from squat to stand position, deep inspiration, and Valsalva, the murmur diminishes but does not disappear; PMI MCL unchanged from last year

Lungs: Clear to auscultation and percussion

Abdominal: Soft, nontender; no hepatosplenomegaly

Extremities: No cyanosis, clubbing, or edema; strength and sensation are symmetrical; full range of motion is present in neck, shoulders, elbows, wrists, hands, back, hips, knees, and ankles

After reviewing the case and the Grading Criteria in Appendix A, jot down your notes or preliminary answers in the spaces provided below. When you are ready to submit your answers for grading (if you are working with an instructor) and reflective feedback to help you evaluate your answers, go to **http://www.evolve.elsevier.com/Cappiello/** to complete this case.

Learning Issues

Before identifying your recommended Assessment and Plan, identify any learning issues that you believe are important for you to explore about this case:

Assessment

Please indicate the problems or issues you have identified that will guide your care (preferably in list form):

Plan

Please list your plans for addressing each of the problems or issues in your assessment:

Case 29

Henry ("Hank") Dodge
Age 83

Opening Scenario

On your schedule today is Henry ("Hank") Dodge, an 83-year-old male. He is scheduled for a six-month follow-up. He had been seeing a physician who recently left the practice where you work. He is here alone. He tells you, "My stamina is not as good as it used to be. I think I am also getting a bit more forgetful."

History of Present Illness

In response to your questions he offers the following answers:
- Walks half a mile a day
- Does not test sugars—"never could figure that machine out"
- No chest pain, no shortness of breath; stamina has decreased gradually over past several years
- Got his previsit laboratory tests as requested

Medical History

T2DM diagnosed at age 55
Atrial fibrillation diagnosed at age 72 (sees cardiologist every six months)
Last colonoscopy was three years ago; they found a tubular adenoma and recommended a 5-year follow-up
Cataract surgery bilaterally with implants 10 years ago
Immunization history: Pneumovax 23 at age 65; Tdap 8 years ago; declined shingles shot, too expensive, "my insurance doesn't cover it"; gets annual flu shot

Family Medical History

Mother: Deceased around age 60 (had "some kind of cancer")
Father: Deceased at age 75 (stroke)
Brother: 87 years old, MI ×2 (former smoker)
Son: 59 years old, HTN and prostate issues

Grandchildren: Janet Jones, 37 years old (has multiple sclerosis, is a physical therapist, comes to this practice); Jennifer, 35 years old, college professor of sociology; and Joan, 30 years old, stays at home with her two young daughters

Social History

Lives with wife, who is 82 years old; married 60 years
Worked as a parts manager at a local car dealership for many years
Smoking: Smoked two years, but hasn't smoked for 40+ years
ETOH: None
Economic: Has Medicare A, B, and D; also Medi-Gap policy
Rarely active sexually

Functional Assessment

Lives in same home for 30+ years; no tub rail or toilet bars
Continues to drive; wife does shopping
Activities: Son lives 30 miles away, visits about once a month; one granddaughter (Janet) who lives about 15 minutes away
Sleeps about 5½ hours per night and takes about two-hour nap in the afternoon most days
Nutrition: 24-hour recall—English muffin and coffee for breakfast; soup and sandwich for lunch; meat, potato, and vegetables for supper; snack in the evening
Culture: ⅟₃₂ Penobscot Indian, half French-Canadian
Religion: "Home Baptist"
Education history: Finished high school
Smoke detectors in house
Uses seatbelt

Medications

Rivaroxaban, 20 mg daily *prevents blood clots* *has AFib*
Lisinopril, 5 mg daily *ace- high BP*
Metoprolol, XL 50 mg daily *treat high BP*
Baby aspirin, 81 mg daily *blood thinner*
Tamsulosin, 0.4 mg at bedtime *enlarged prostate*
Miralax, 1 capful daily *constipation*

Allergies

Muscle aching with trial of simvastatin several years ago
A little hay fever sometimes
NKDA

Review of Systems

General: Denies night sweats, swelling; denies anorexia, nausea, vomiting

HEENT: Denies diplopia; cataract surgeries with implants 10 years ago; mild hearing impairment; denies sore throat

Respiratory: Denies chest pain, shortness of breath, dyspnea on exertion, and paroxysmal nocturnal dyspnea

Gastrointestinal: Occasional constipation, takes milk of magnesia 30 mL when constipated; takes Miralax every day to "keep regular"; denies diarrhea, black or clay-colored stools, dysuria, hematuria;

Genitourinary: Sometimes a little hesitancy starting stream "but not too bad"; up two times per night to urinate; sometimes a little bright-red blood on the toilet paper (for years)

Cardiovascular: Denies excessive bruising; no transfusion history

Physical Examination

Vital signs: Temperature 97.4° F; pulse 68 bpm; respirations 22/min; BP 128/84 mm Hg

Height: 5 ft 8 in; *weight:* 177 lb; *BMI:* 26.9

HEENT: Normocephalic, atraumatic; pupils equal, round, and reactive to light; extra-ocular membranes are intact; tympanic membranes are blocked with cerumen; nares are patent without redness or exudate; throat is noninjected; tongue is midline, palate rises symmetrically, teeth are in adequate repair

Neck: Supple without thyromegaly, adenopathy, or carotid bruits

Heart: Irregularly irregular but without murmurs, rubs, or gallops

Lungs: Clear to auscultation and percussion

Abdominal: Soft, nontender; no hepatosplenomegaly

Rectal: Brown stool, no masses; prostate is mildly enlarged but symmetrical and without nodules; FIT is negative

Genitalia: Normal externally

Extremities: No cyanosis, clubbing, or edema

Neurological: Reflexes are 2+ at the biceps, triceps, brachioradialis, patellar; Achilles reflexes are absent bilaterally; Babinskis are not present; strength and sensation are symmetrical

Laboratory Tests for Henry ("Hank") Dodge

Blood (drawn three days ago)

CBC	Results	Normal Values
WBC	8.2	4.5–10.8
RBC	4.45	4.20–5.40

Hgb	11.9 L	12.0–16.0
Hct	36.2 L	37.0–47.0
MCV	98.3	81.0–99.0
MCH	31.2	27.0–32.0
MCHC	33.4	32.0–36.0
RDW	15.2	11.0–16.0
Platelets	221	150–450
Segs	64	50–65
Lymphs	29	25–45
Monos	9	0–10
Eos	4	0–4

Chemistry profile (from three days ago)

	Results	Normal Values
FBS	116 H	60–100
BUN	20	8–28
Creatinine	1.0	0.5–1.5
Sodium	137	135–145
Potassium	4.3	3.5–5.5
Chloride	104	95–105
Albumin	4.2	4.0–6.0
Total protein	6.6	6.5–8.0
Alk phos	130 H	30–120
ALT	22	0–40
AST	28	0–40
LDH	134	50–150
Calcium	9.0	8.8–10.2
GGT	29	0–30
Magnesium	2.1	1.6–2.4
Bilirubin	0.7	0.1–1.0
Conjugated bilirubin	0.1	0.0–0.2

Iron	61	60–160
Uric acid	6.3	2.0–7.0
HgbA1C	7.2	
Microalbumin	20 mg	

Urinalysis (drawn three days ago)

	Results
Color	Yellow
Character	Clear
s.g.	1.015
Urine pH	5.5
Glucose	Negative
Nitrite	Negative
Protein	Negative
WBCs	0–2
RBCs	0–1
Epithelial cells	0–5
Crystals	None

Lipid profile (three days ago)

	Results
Total cholesterol	220
HDL	41
Triglycerides	188
LDL	141
Risk ratio	5.37

Chest x-ray (obtained today)

The lung fields are clear of infiltrates. The pulmonary vasculature and markings are normal. The heart size is within normal limits.
Impression: Normal chest x-ray.
Julio Sanchez, MD

Mini-Cog administered: Registration 3/3. Recall 3/3. Clock drawing normal.

After reviewing the case and the Grading Criteria in Appendix A, jot down your notes or preliminary answers in the spaces provided below. When you are ready to submit your answers for grading (if you are working with an instructor) and reflective feedback to help you evaluate your answers, go to **http://www.evolve.elsevier.com/Cappiello/** to complete this case.

Learning Issues

Before identifying your recommended Assessment and Plan, identify any learning issues that you believe are important for you to explore about this case:

Assessment

Please indicate the problems or issues you have identified that will guide your care (preferably in list form):

Plan

Please list your plans for addressing each of the problems or issues in your assessment:

Case 30

Deborah Pierce
Age 39 years

Opening Scenario

Deborah Pierce is a 39-year-old female in your office with a three-week history of back pain.

History of Present Illness

"My back pain has been bothering me for about three weeks. I don't remember a specific episode initiating the onset. I work as a toll taker on the turnpike, and this aggravates the pain. The pain is across my entire low back and right buttock, going down into the back of my right thigh. I have no numbness or tingling." Ms. Pierce has tried Motrin 800 mg every 6 hours that she had at home for dysmenorrhea, and "it has not done anything." There is some relief with lying down and putting ice on her back, then it is just a dull ache. Pain is a 7 on a scale of 0 to 10 when she is moving around. Pain is at its worst later in the day after she works. States that she "never had back pain like this before."

Medical History

Kidney stone two years ago. Treated with lithotripsy.

Family Medical History

Not available

Social History

Lives with boyfriend. One glass of wine each day. Smokes one-half pack per day.

Medications

Motrin: 800 mg every 6 hours prn

Allergies

Percocet makes her sick to her stomach.

Review of Systems

Gastrointestinal: Denies nausea, vomiting
Genitourinary: Denies dysuria, hematuria

Physical Examination

Vital signs: Temperature 98.4° F; pulse 88 bpm; respirations 22/min; BP 142/84 mm Hg
Height: 5 ft 6 in; *weight:* 224 lb
Painful area: No external lesions or masses; tension of paraspinal muscles palpable; no
  excessive warmth; generally tender over low back; no tenderness specific to costovertebral angle
Gross sensory testing: Sensation present and normal along the L_4, L_5, and S_1 derma-
  tomes
Straight-leg raises (SLRs): Pain occurs in low back on right at 30 degrees, but there is no
  pain in the legs; pain occurs on left at 45 degrees with some pain in the posterior
  thigh; no shooting pain or paresthesias into calf on raising her head during SLRs
Extremities: Reflexes 2+ at patella bilaterally, 1+ at Achilles bilaterally, no Babinski signs
  present; range of motion: Side bending 30 degrees bilaterally, flexion 20 degrees,
  extension 5 degrees, rotation 10 degrees bilaterally without pain; strength testing:
  4/5 bilaterally with foot dorsiflexion and plantar flexion; gait: Antalgic (obviously
  painful) and slow but symmetrical and steady; able to do heel walk and toe walk;
  no pain in back on compression downward on top of head
Genitourinary: Urine dip negative (SG 1.015)

After reviewing the case and the Grading Criteria in Appendix A, jot down your notes or preliminary answers in the spaces provided below. When you are ready to submit your answers for grading (if you are working with an instructor) and reflective feedback to help you evaluate your answers, go to **http://www.evolve.elsevier.com/Cappiello/** to complete this case.

Learning Issues

Before identifying your recommended Assessment and Plan, identify any learning issues that you believe are important for you to explore about this case:

Assessment

Please indicate the problems or issues you have identified that will guide your care (preferably in list form):

Plan

Please list your plans for addressing each of the problems or issues in your assessment:

Case 31

Mimi Murray
Age 54 years

Opening Scenario

Mimi Murray is a 54-year-old woman who comes to your office to establish care with a new practice/primary care provider because her previous provider retired about one year ago. Her primary concern is that she noticed some chest tightness for a couple of days last week. She brought her records from her gynecologist. Medical records have also been requested from her prior primary care provider.

History of Present Illness

"I had some chest tightness last week but it was just noticeable, not truly uncomfortable. It happened during the daytime one day last week. I was not doing anything physical, just sitting. It was not a sharp pain or burning, just a tight feeling that lasted for a few seconds but then stayed constant over several days as I went about my daily routine. I have not had symptoms this week. I went to see my gynecologist yesterday for my regularly scheduled visit. She thought I should have this evaluated and referred me here."

The patient denies pain radiation to her jaw, neck, shoulders, arms, back, or upper abdomen. No numbness of the arms, pain with movement, or diaphoresis. No palpitations, lightheadedness, or dizziness. No pain with deep breathing or coughing. No recent URI. The discomfort did not keep her awake. No nausea or symptoms related to eating. Has no history of reflux disease, cholecystitis, or peptic ulcer disease. No history of trauma to the chest, heavy lifting, or change of exercise regimen at the gym. Has not noticed any tenderness on the chest wall.

She has been on metoprolol 25 mg bid for five years for high blood pressure. When she developed this discomfort last week, she increased her metoprolol to 50 mg in the morning and 25 mg in the evening. She did not notice any change in the discomfort. When she was first put on metoprolol, she used this dose but felt better on the 25 mg bid, so the dose was reduced.

She usually exercises regularly, but in the last three weeks she has been too busy and has not been doing any exercise.

Medical History

Hypertension for five years. Left breast cyst removed six years ago. Cryosurgery for abnormal Pap smears (atypical squamous cells of undetermined significance [ASCUS]) four years ago. No history of myocardial infarction, cerebrovascular accident, or diabetes mellitus.

Family Medical History

Mother: Deceased at age 78 (ovarian cancer)
Father: Deceased at age 71 (lung cancer)
Ten siblings: One sister with hypertension; others healthy as far as she knows; Ms. Murray is the oldest

Social History

Smoking for 30 years at 1½ packs per day. Has tried to quit on numerous occasions but always relapses. Alcohol use: three to four glasses of wine per day. Caffeine: two cups of tea per day. Lives with husband. Two grown sons are both married. Adopted a 14-year-old child with special needs six years ago. Much stress with him over the past six months, although he now lives on his own. Joined a meditation group six months ago, meditates three times a week for 30 minutes. She is a writer and owns a marketing agency with her husband.

Medications

Metoprolol 50 mg in morning, 25 mg in evening
Daily multivitamin
Chinese herbs

Allergies

NKDA

Review of Systems

General: Usually feels very healthy; weight slowly increasing, approximately 40 pounds over the past 10 years; no recent changes; sleeps seven to eight hours per night and feels rested during the day
Integumentary: Has not noticed any rashes, lesions
HEENT: Denies problems with allergies; no visual changes other than wears reading glasses; denies tinnitus, vertigo, pain, discharge; no nosebleeds, discharge, sinus problems; gum surgery for gingivitis one year ago; no hoarseness, sore throat, pain; states she has not had a cold in 15 years because she uses high doses of vitamin C (1500 to 2000 mg) per day if she feels symptomatic

Cardiovascular: Denies chest pain; just tightness as described under History of Present Illness

Respiratory: Denies asthma, shortness of breath

Breasts: Yearly mammograms since breast biopsy 6 years ago; does breast self-examination

Gastrointestinal: Denies heartburn, stomach, epigastric, or abdominal pain; no constipation, diarrhea, hemorrhoids, or recent bowel changes

Genitourinary: Review of gynecological records: G2P2; menopause began four years ago; two years ago had light bleeding for one week after two years without menses; endometrial biopsy showed scant tissue; no bleeding since and did not have the endometrial biopsy repeated; takes Chinese herbs daily (prescribed by an acupuncturist) that have controlled hot flashes to an infrequent basis at this point; is still taking a daily maintenance dose; has a yearly pelvic sonogram because of her mother's history of ovarian cancer; refuses hormone replacement therapy (HRT) because of mother's history of ovarian cancer; Pap smears within normal limits since cryosurgery four years ago; most recent Pap smear six months ago

Musculoskeletal: Fracture of right ankle four years ago; bone density testing two years ago

Endocrine: Rare headaches; temperature tolerances good; no arthralgias or myalgias

Neurological: Headaches rarely

Physical Examination

Vital signs: Temperature 98.0° F; pulse 70 bpm; respirations 16/min; BP 140/90 mm Hg

Height: 5 ft 9 in; *weight:* 185; *BMI:* 27.3

General: Healthy, alert, calm 54-year-old woman who looks her stated age

Skin: No rashes, lesions, bruising

HEENT: Pupils equal and reactive to light; funduscopic examination reveals normal arteries and veins bilaterally with no arteriovenous nicking or focal constrictions; extraocular movements intact; no discharge in ears, crisp cone of light, landmarks visualized; nose reveals no discharge or polyps; oropharynx is moist without lesions

Neck: Supple without adenopathy, thyromegaly, jugular venous distention, or bruits

Heart: Regular rate and rhythm; no murmurs, rubs, or gallops; no discomfort elicited with pressure on costochondral joint

Lungs: Clear to auscultation bilaterally

Breast: Deferred

Abdomen: Soft, nontender, without masses; no hepatosplenomegaly or bruit; no epigastric or right upper quadrant tenderness; negative costovertebral angle tenderness

Genitourinary: Pelvic deferred

Extremities: Negative for cyanosis, clubbing, or edema; no redness, phlebitis; pedal pulses palpable and equal bilaterally

Neurological: Normal gait; cranial nerves 2 to 12 intact; biceps, triceps, patellar, ankle deep tendon reflexes: 2+

Office electrocardiogram (ECG) performed today (Figure 31-1). The laboratory tests shown in Tables 31-1 to 31-4 and Box 31-1 were ordered by her gynecologist this week and faxed to you.

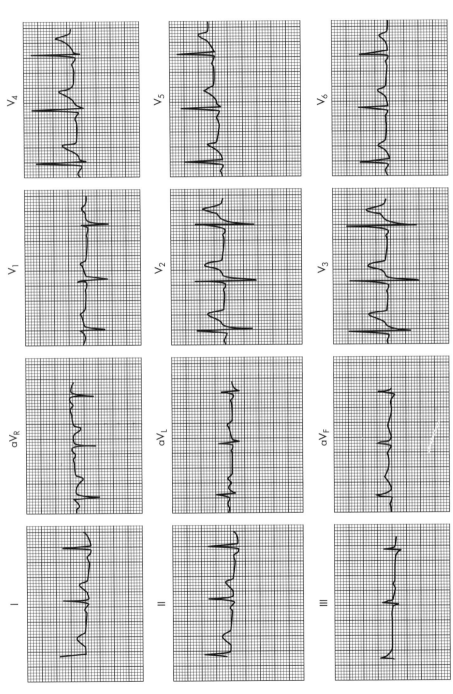

Figure 31-1 Results of Mimi Murray's ECG. (From Kinney, M. R., & Packa, D. R. [1996]. *Andreoli's comprehensive cardiac care* [8th ed.] St Louis, MO: Mosby.)

TABLE 31-1 Chemistry Panel CP-12 for Mimi Murray

Test	Result	Reference Value
Glucose	104 mg/dL	65–115
BUN	12 mg/dL	16–26
Creatinine	0.7 mg/dL	0.5–1.3
Calcium	9.4 mg/dL	8.2–10.2
Uric acid	6.1 mg/dL	2.5–6.6
Total protein	7.2 g/dL	6.2–8.3
Albumin	4.4 g/dL	3.4–5.2
Bilirubin, total	0.4 mg/dL	0.0–1.2
Alkaline phosphatase	100 U/L	0–125
AST (SGOT)	25 U/L	0–40
ALT (SGPT)	36	0–40
LDH	144 U/L	0–230

TABLE 31-2 Cardiac Risk/Lipid Profile for Mimi Murray

Test	Result	Reference Value
Cholesterol, total	314 mg/dL	<200
Triglycerides	195 mg/dL	<150
Cholesterol, HDL	54 mg/dL	>35
Cholesterol, LDL	221 mg/dL	<130
Cholesterol/HDL ratio	5.8	<4.44
CHD relative risk ratio	1.6 × average	Average risk = 1.0
LDL/HDL risk	4.1	<3.22
CHD relative risk ratio	1.4 × average	Average risk = 1.0

TABLE 31-3 Complete Blood Count for Mimi Murray

Test	Result	Reference Value
WBC	5.2 × 1000/mL	3.9–9.9
RBC	4.56 million/mL	4.2–5.4
Hemoglobin	14.9 g/dL	12.0–16.0
Hematocrit	44.7%	37.0–47.0
MCV	98.1 fl	81.0–99.0
MCH	32.7 pg	27.0–31.0
MCHC	33.3 g/dL	33.0–37.0
RDW	12.5%	11.5–14.5
Platelet count	207 × 1000/mL	130–451
MPV	8.5 fl	7.0–12.0
Lymphocyte %	40.4%	20.0–45.0
Monocyte %	4.5%	0.2–8.0
Granulocyte %	55.1%	42.0–80.0
Lymphocytes	2.1 × 1000/mL	1.2–4.5
Monocytes	0.2 × 1000 /mL	0.1–0.6
Granulocytes	2.9 × 1000/mL	1.4–9.9
Eosinophils	0.7 × 1000/mL	0.0–0.7
Basophils	0.2 × 1000/mL	0.0–0.2

TABLE 31-4   Urinalysis for Mimi Murray

Test	Result	Reference Value
Color	Yellow	
Appearance	Clear	
Specific gravity	1.015	1.003–1.029
pH	5.5	4.5–8.0
Protein	Negative	
Glucose	Negative	
Ketones	Negative	
Nitrite	Negative	
Bilirubin	Negative	
Urobilinogen	1.0	0.2–1.0
Leukocytes	Negative	

BOX 31-1   Bone Densitometry Report

Ms. Murray is a 54-year-old white woman who appears to eat calcium products regularly and does regular aerobics. She does, however, smoke 1½ packs of cigarettes per day, and she apparently is on no medications except a beta blocker and various herbs and vitamins. She takes no specific calcium supplement. She has lost no height and has had three pregnancies. She stopped menstruating 2 years ago, and she had a chip fracture of her foot at age 50. There is no family history of osteoporosis.

Bone density report at this time is approximately 2 years after menopause and shows her hip to be about average for a patient in her age group and to be on the average 0.8 standard deviation (SD) below patients at peak bone mass throughout the hip. However, at the femoral neck, the most critical area for fracture, she is 1.42 SD below peak bone mass.

As far as her vertebral spine is concerned, on the average she is 110% of what you would expect to see in her age group and 101% of what you would expect to see at peak bone mass.

IMPRESSION: The patient's bone mass at her femoral neck is somewhat worrisome in that it is greater than 1 SD below someone at peak bone mass, suggesting mild osteopenia. She also has a mildly enlarged hip axis of 11.143 cm, which also increases her risk of hip fracture supposedly on just a structural basis.

My own personal feeling would be that, based on the patient's hip structure and her mild osteoporosis at the femoral neck, estrogen replacement therapy should be considered because she is still in the accelerated phase of bone loss. If I were not anxious to treat her with estrogen, I would suggest that she be reevaluated in 2 years.

Thank you for allowing me to read the bone densitometry report on Ms. Murray.

Sincerely,

Harold Xavier, MD

After reviewing the case and the Grading Criteria in Appendix A, jot down your notes or preliminary answers in the spaces provided below. When you are ready to submit your answers for grading (if you are working with an instructor) and reflective feedback to help you evaluate your answers, go to **http://www.evolve.elsevier.com/Cappiello/** to complete this case.

Learning Issues

Before identifying your recommended Assessment and Plan, identify any learning issues that you believe are important for you to explore about this case:

Assessment

Please indicate the problems or issues you have identified that will guide your care (preferably in list form):

Plan

Please list your plans for addressing each of the problems or issues in your assessment:

Al Olsson
Age 55 years

Opening Scenario

Mr. Olsson is a 55-year-old man scheduled for an episodic visit for pain in his left big toe. He was seen once previously for a physical in your office 3½ years ago.

History of Present Illness

"Yesterday I awoke with pain in my left big toe. I don't remember injuring my foot in any way. I have not had anything like this previously. It bothers my toe to wear shoes. The pain is intense and has not improved since yesterday except when I took two extra-strength acetaminophen, which gave me some relief." The patient denies fever or chills.

Medical History

Three months ago his lipid profile showed an opportunity for improvement (total cholesterol 198, high-density lipoprotein 50, low-density lipoprotein 128, triglycerides 103). He states he is improving his diet and increasing his exercise level. History of hypertension for three years. Well controlled on medication. No history of diabetes mellitus, arthritis, or other joint disorders. No hospitalizations or surgeries.

Family Medical History

Mother: 79 years old (type 2 diabetes mellitus, onset age 70 years)
Father: Died at age 84 (MI)
Sister: 50 years old (A&W)
Brother: 57 years old (HTN)

Social History

Married, husband has human immunodeficiency virus (HIV). Works long hours as an insurance agent. Nonsmoker for three years, previously smoked ¾ pack per day for

22 years. Drinks one glass of wine with dinner each night. Walks one-half mile each day on his lunch hour. Has not made any significant diet changes since last visit when told his lipids were elevated.

Medications

Lisinopril 20 mg
Truvada (emtricitabine 200 mg and 300 mg of tenofovir disoproxil fumarate 300 mg)

Allergies

NKDA

Review of Systems

General: Often tired from long days of working but rests on the weekends and feels better; weight up 20 lb in past five years
Integumentary: Denies any skin problems such as rashes, bruising, skin discoloration
HEENT: No upper respiratory infection or bronchitis since stopped smoking 3 years ago; wears reading glasses; regular dental care
Cardiovascular: No chest pain or history of cardiac problems, hypertension well-controlled
Respiratory: Denies cough, shortness of breath
Gastrointestinal: No nausea, vomiting, constipation, diarrhea, blood in stools
Genitourinary: Occasional nocturia and loss of force of stream
Endocrine: Denies change of skin or hair; temperature tolerances good
Musculoskeletal: No fractures; occasional low backaches if sitting all day; does not take any medication for this because it is mild; no recent fracture or trauma to left foot, sprained left ankle 10 years ago but no problems with it since; no history of gout or any type of arthritis.
Neurological: Denies weakness, paresthesias

Physical Examination

Vital signs: Temperature 98.4° F; pulse 74 bpm; respirations 20/min; BP 136/72 mm Hg
Height: 5 ft 10 in; *weight:* 205 lb; *BMI:* 29
Left foot: No redness, swelling, or pain to palpation; no bony deformities noted
Right foot: First metatarsophalangeal joint is erythematous, edematous, tender to palpation; no crepitus; ankle range of motion limited because of pain; no bony deformity noted; no pain palpated in midfoot, ankle, knee; no tophi noted

After reviewing the case and the Grading Criteria in Appendix A, jot down your notes or preliminary answers in the spaces provided below. When you are ready to submit your answers for grading (if you are working with an instructor) and reflective feedback to help you evaluate your answers, go to http://www.evolve.elsevier.com/Cappiello/ to complete this case.

Learning Issues

Before identifying your recommended Assessment and Plan, identify any learning issues that you believe are important for you to explore about this case:

Assessment

Please indicate the problems or issues you have identified that will guide your care (preferably in list form):

Plan

Please list your plans for addressing each of the problems or issues in your assessment:

Case 33

Rose D'Angelo
Age 78 years

Opening Scenario

Rose D'Angelo is a 78-year-old female on your schedule for a new patient complete physical examination.

History of Present Illness

"My granddaughter thought I should have a physical. *[She had called ahead and a colleague had ordered some laboratory tests.]* My back aches a lot, and my right hip has been bothering me too. My back has been bothering me for years. It's worse if I do a lot during the day. Tylenol makes it a little better but not much. I'd rate it a 6 on a scale of 0 to 10. It's mostly an ache, but it feels kind of sharp sometimes. It's in my back and deep in my right hip. The back pain came on first about 15 years ago. It has gradually been getting worse over the years. The hip pain started last year, and it has also gradually been getting worse." Ms. D'Angelo denies radiation down the leg, other associated symptoms, saddle paresthesias, bowel and bladder changes, and trauma.

Medical History

Has not been to a provider in about 20 years. Only problems before that were coughs and colds. Obstetrical history: One child, now 60 years old; two miscarriages after that.

Family Medical History

Parents: Died years ago (both over 80 years old of "natural causes"); does not remember the years that they died
Father's sister: Died young (possible DM)
Brother: 83 years old (stroke; is aphasic)
Sister: 80 years old (HTN)
Brother: 77 years old (high cholesterol)
Sister: 76 years old (type 2 DM and hypertension)

Daughter: 60 years old (A&W)
Three granddaughters: 30, 35, and 37 years old (A&W)

Social History

Husband died about five years ago of sudden cardiac event. He stayed active until his death. He was 80 years old. She never worked other than at the chicken farm that she and her husband owned. They sold it and moved near the ocean 35 years ago (100+ miles from here). About six months ago, her granddaughters talked her into moving into an apartment near here. One lives here in town, one about a half hour away, and one about 45 minutes away. Daughter lives about 15 minutes away. Never smoked. Drinks wine whenever the family gets together (about once a month).

Economic: Has Medicare A, B, and D and a Medigap policy; has investments that provide for her; collects social security from her husband's benefit; reticent about discussing. Not currently active sexually.

Lives in an apartment with three steps at the entrance. Has a handrail. Apartment is all on one floor. No bathtub rail or toilet bars. Continues to drive her car but does not drive at night. Does her own shopping. Has a washer and dryer in her apartment. Goes on trips with the Senior Center, takes a ceramics class weekly, gets hair done weekly. Sleeps about 7½ hours per night and takes a one-hour nap in the afternoon most days. Nutrition: 24-hour recall—fruit and coffee for breakfast, a sandwich for lunch, meat and vegetables for dinner, snack in the evening. Culture: First-generation Italian; husband was born in Italy; he came over to the United States at age 13. Religion: Roman Catholic; attends mass sometimes, other times watches on television. Education: Finished elementary school, then worked in her parents store until she got married. Smoke detectors in her apartment. Does not use her seatbelt very often.

Medications

Vitamin C, 2000 mg per day
Vitamin E, 400 IU per day
Zinc, one tablet (unknown mg)

Allergies

A little hay fever sometimes, NKDA

Review of Systems

General: Denies night sweats, swelling; says energy level is good
HEENT: Denies diplopia; notes occasional blurring; some hearing impairment; denies
    sore throats

Cardiovascular: Denies chest pain; no peripheral edema; denies excessive bruising; no history of transfusion

Respiratory: Denies shortness of breath, dyspnea on exertion, and paroxysmal nocturnal dyspnea

Gastrointestinal: Denies anorexia, nausea, vomiting; occasional constipation (takes a laxative about twice a week and takes Metamucil every day to stay regular); denies diarrhea, black or clay-colored stools; sometimes a little bright red blood on the toilet paper

Genitourinary: Denies dysuria, hematuria; leaks a little urine rarely when she coughs or sneezes

Physical Examination

Vital signs: Temperature 97.1° F; pulse 88 bpm; respirations 22/min; BP 148/84 mm Hg

Height: 5 ft 3 in; *weight:* 170 lb; *BMI:* 30.1

HEENT: Head is normocephalic, atraumatic; pupils equal, round, and reactive to light; extraocular movements intact; tympanic membranes observable without excessive cerumen; nares patent without redness or exudate; throat is noninjected; tongue is midline; palate rises symmetrically; teeth in adequate repair

Neck: Supple without thyromegaly, adenopathy, or carotid bruits

Heart: Regular rate and rhythm; no murmurs, rubs, or gallops

Lungs: Clear to auscultation and percussion

Breasts: Without dimpling, discharge, or masses

Abdomen: Soft, nontender; no hepatosplenomegaly

Gastrointestinal: Brown stool, no masses, small external hemorrhoidal tags

Genitourinary: Normal externally; pelvic examination refused

Extremities: Without cyanosis, clubbing, or edema

Neurological: Reflexes are 2+ at the biceps, triceps, brachioradialis, patellar; Achilles reflexes are absent bilaterally; Babinski signs are not present; strength and sensation are symmetrical; Folstein administered: Loss of point for county, loss of one point for recall; no other deductions: 28/30

See Tables 33-1 to 33-3 and Box 33-1 for laboratory results for Ms. D'Angelo.

TABLE 33-1 Complete Blood Count for Rose D'Angelo

CBC	Result	Normal Range
WBC	8.2 3 1000/mL	4.5–10.8
RBC	4.45 million/mL	4.20–5.40
Hgb	13.9 g/dL	12.0–16.0
Hct	38.2%	37.0–47.0
MCV	98.3 fl	81.0–99.0
MCH	31.2 pg	27.0–32.0
MCHC	33.4 g/dL	32.0–36.0
RDW	15.2%	11.0–16.0
Platelets	221 3 1000/mL	150–450
Segs	64%	50–65
Lymphocytes	23%	25–45
Monocytes	9%	0–10
Eosinophils	4%	0–4

TABLE 33-3 Urinalysis for Rose D'Angelo

Color	Yellow
Character	Clear
Specific gravity	1.015
Urine pH	5.5
Glucose	Negative
Nitrite	Negative
WBCs	0–2
RBCs	0–1
Epithelial cells	0–5
Crystals	None

TABLE 33-2 Chemistry Profile for Rose D'Angelo

Test	Result	Normal Range
FBS	101	60–100
BUN	20 mg/dL	18–28
Creatinine	1.0 mg/dL	0.5–1.5
Sodium	137	135–145
Potassium	4.3	3.5–5.5
Chloride	104	95–105
Albumin	4.2 g/dL	4.0–6.0
Total protein	6.6 g/dL	6.5–8.0
Alkaline phosphatase	100 U/L	30–120
ALT (SGPT)	22	0–40
AST (SGOT)	28 U/L	0–40
LDH	134 U/L	50–150
Cholesterol	220 mg/dL	110–200
Calcium	9.0 mg/dL	8.8–10.2
GGT	29	0–30
Magnesium	2.1	1.6–2.4
Bilirubin	0.7 mg/dL	0.1–1.0
Conjugated bilirubin	0.1	0.0–0.2
Iron	61	60–160
Uric acid	6.3 mg/dL	2.0–7.0

BOX 33-1 Chest X-Ray Examination for Rose D'Angelo

The lung fields are clear of infiltrates. The pulmonary vasculature and markings are normal. The heart size is within normal limits.

Impression: Normal chest x-ray.

Boyd Bates, DO

After reviewing the case and the Grading Criteria in Appendix A, jot down your notes or preliminary answers in the spaces provided below. When you are ready to submit your answers for grading (if you are working with an instructor) and reflective feedback to help you evaluate your answers, go to http://www.evolve.elsevier.com/Cappiello/ to complete this case.

Learning Issues

Before identifying your recommended Assessment and Plan, identify any learning issues that you believe are important for you to explore about this case:

Assessment

Please indicate the problems or issues you have identified that will guide your care (preferably in list form):

Plan

Please list your plans for addressing each of the problems or issues in your assessment:

Case 34

Lisa Pacheco

Age 9 months

Opening Scenario

Lisa Pacheco is a nine-month-old infant girl on your schedule for diarrhea for five days.

History of Present Illness

(Obtained from mother)

"Lisa had a runny nose and cough about one week ago, and her stuffiness seems to be getting better. She started with diarrhea about five days ago, and that is still present. She had one episode of vomiting about five days ago but none since. Her stools are almost pure brown liquid, and she has about four to five per day. She seems a little uncomfortable just before she moves her bowels and seems to act like she feels better after she goes. She is feeding and drinking well. She is nursing, and I have been giving her cheese and bananas hoping it would bind her up. She is urinating about four to five times a day, which is her normal pattern. She is getting a little diaper rash. She attends family day care five days per week. Her older sister has no symptoms."

Medical History

No accidents or hospitalizations. Immunization record is shown in Table 34-1.

Family Medical History

Father: 24 years old (smokes one pack cigarettes/day, A&W)
Mother: 23 years old (A&W)
Sister: 3 years old (A&W)
MGM, MGF, PGM, PGF – (A&W)

Medications

None

TABLE 34-1 Immunization Record for Lisa Pacheco

Vaccine	Date	Initials	Notes
Hep B #1	Birth		
Hep B #2	2 mo	MDO	
Hep B #3			
RV5 #1	2 mo	MDO	
RV5 #2	4 mo	KJ	
RV5 #3	6 mo	SP	
DTaP #1	2 mo	MDO	
DTaP #2	4 mo	KJ	
DTaP #3	6 mo	SP	
DTaP #4			
DTaP #5			
Tdap			
Hib #1	2 mo	MDO	
Hib #2	4 mo	KJ	
Hib #3			
PCV13 #1	2 mo	MDO	
PCV13 #2	4 mo	KJ	
PCV13 #3	6 mo	SP	
PCV13 #4			
IPV #1	2 mo	MDO	
IPV #2	4 mo	KJ	
IPV #3	6 mo	SP	
IPV #4			
MMR #1			
MMR #2			
Varicella #1			
Varicella #2			
Hep A #1			
Hep A #2			

Allergies

NKDA

Review of Systems

(Obtained from mother)
General: No night sweats
Cardiovascular: No evidence of dyspnea, swelling. No excessive bruising
Gastrointestinal: No anorexia, nausea, vomiting, black or clay-colored stools
Genitourinary: No hematuria or pain

Physical Examination

Vital signs: Temperature 98.6° F (tympanic); pulse 108 bpm; respirations 25/min
Height: 28 in; *weight:* 18.5 lb (6-month check: 32 in, 16.5 lb)
Skin: Intact in rectal area; mild to moderate perirectal redness (about 3 cm in diameter); no satellite lesions seen; skin turgor without skin tenting
HEENT: Head is normocephalic, anterior fontanel is flat; pupils equal, round, and reactive to light; extraocular movements intact; eyes moist, tympanic membranes translucent and mobile; nares are patent without redness or exudate; throat is noninjected; tongue midline; mouth moist; palate rises symmetrically; all three teeth are in adequate repair
Neck: Supple without thyromegaly or adenopathy
Heart: Regular rate and rhythm; no murmurs, rubs, or gallops
Respiratory: Clear to auscultation and percussion
Abdominal: Soft, nontender; no hepatosplenomegaly
Extremities: Without cyanosis, clubbing, or edema; capillary refill brisk
Neuromuscular: Babinski reflexes are equivocal; strength and sensation are symmetrical

After reviewing the case and the Grading Criteria in Appendix A, jot down your notes or preliminary answers in the spaces provided below. When you are ready to submit your answers for grading (if you are working with an instructor) and reflective feedback to help you evaluate your answers, go to **http://www.evolve.elsevier.com/Cappiello/** to complete this case.

Learning Issues

Before identifying your recommended Assessment and Plan, identify any learning issues that you believe are important for you to explore about this case:

Assessment

Please indicate the problems or issues you have identified that will guide your care (preferably in list form):

Plan

Please list your plans for addressing each of the problems or issues in your assessment:

Case 35

Lynne Spencer

Age 19 years

Opening Scenario

Lynne Spencer is a 19-year-old, single, female college sophomore scheduled for refill of her oral contraceptives. This is her first visit to your practice. She is slumped in her chair and appears tired.

History of Present Illness

"I'm here for renewal of birth control pills. Since the beginning of the semester, I've been feeling depressed and increasingly stressed. Much of this stress is due to financial concerns because I need a job to pay tuition. Last summer I had a good work-study job that I really liked, but it did not carry over into this semester. I don't have friends other than my boyfriend, and we don't seem to have much fun anymore."

Medical History

History of chronic allergies with ongoing sinus and bronchitis problems. Mononucleosis as a high school sophomore. After this, she was diagnosed with systemic exertion intolerance disorder (SEID). Had a series of sinus infections through her junior and senior years resulting in missing a great deal of school, which was difficult socially. Sinus surgery during her senior year with fewer infections since then. History of asthma, controlled currently with cetirizine, beclomethasone dipropionate inhaler daily, and albuterol as needed.

Family Medical History

MGM: 67 years old (HTN)
MGF: 69 years old (emphysema)
PGM: 71 years old (A&W)
PGF: 71 years old (Alzheimer's disease)
Mother: 45 years old (A&W)
Father: 47 years old (chronically depressed)
Sister: 23 years old (A&W)

Social History

Lives in dorm with one roommate; they do not get along. Is afraid to confront her about issues. Has not made many friends; feels that because she does not drink alcohol, she is not popular. Only friends are her boyfriend (some distress over this relationship) and his roommate. Has recently completed a course that will enable her to teach aerobics and is hopeful that this activity will be a way to meet people and earn some money.

Usually visits her parents on the weekend; parents are supportive. Her father is a carpenter who is frequently unemployed because of the seasonal nature of his work. Her mom works in a bank. Her sister just moved to a state far away; she misses her very much. Her father has been chronically depressed since serving in Desert Storm, and it is worse when he is out of work. There is no history of depression on her mother's side of the family.

She denies smoking, alcohol, or drug use. Doing adequately in school, getting B and C grades; had better grades as a freshman. Denies history of domestic violence. Does not use seatbelt.

Complains of difficulty sleeping; stays up late (midnight to 1 AM) because she cannot fall asleep earlier and then wakes frequently during the night. Sometimes she goes back to sleep easily but other times just lies awake feeling sad. Has low energy and feels tired during the day. Rarely takes a daytime nap.

Medications

Cetirizine hydrochloride (Zyrtec): 10 mg daily
Ovcon 35: Daily
Beclomethasone dipropionate (Beclovent) metered dose inhaler: four puffs twice a day
Albuterol (Proventil) inhaler: Two puffs every four hours as needed

Allergies

Environmental allergies, NKDA

Review of Systems

General: States that she has low energy and her mood is low; her weight has been stable for many years
HEENT: Currently no sinus problems of headache, pain, nasal discharge, or postnasal drip, but was treated three months ago with course of cefuroxime, 500 mg twice a day for 10 days with good results; this was her first sinus infection in over one year; sees dentist yearly; no dental problems
Cardiovascular: No chest pain, palpitations, dizziness, or syncope; no history of murmurs
Respiratory: No shortness of breath, difficulty breathing, wheezing, or cough; diagnosed with asthma in high school; uses Beclovent inhaler twice a day without fail

and uses the albuterol inhaler infrequently in the fall and winter; she is bothered more in the summer months with allergies to grasses; uses protective plastic mattress and pillow to protect against dust mites; participates in aerobics without problems; peak flows average 400, which she has not checked since she had the sinus infection

Gastrointestinal: Denies heartburn, abdominal pain, nausea, vomiting, diarrhea, or constipation; appetite less for several weeks, but states she does eat; no weight loss

Genitourinary: Last menstrual period (LMP) was one week ago; on Ovcon 35 for two years; same sexual partner for two years, has known him for five years; denies dyspareunia or postcoital spotting; expresses concerns about lack of sex drive and not having orgasms; denies history of sexual or physical abuse; prior chlamydia screening negative

Endocrine: Low energy; temperature tolerances good; denies dry skin and hair and denies hoarseness.

Neurological: Tension headaches one to two times per week relieved by acetaminophen; saw psychiatrist for two visits during her senior year in high school for insomnia and depression after sinus surgery and slow recovery; no medications or follow-up at that time; states that she fleetingly feels suicidal with no real plans; knows she would never do it because her elementary school teacher committed suicide, and she saw what distress this caused the friends and family of the teacher; feels unhappy with self, insecure; has few close friends

Extremities: No history of fractures, sprains; denies current arthralgias, myalgias

Physical Examination

Vital signs: Temperature 97.8° F; pulse 74 bpm; respirations 16/min; BP 120/76 mm Hg

Height: 5 ft 5 in; *weight:* 125 lb; *BMI:* 21

General: Flat affect; speech a bit slow; mood low

HEENT: No frontal or maxillary pain elicited; nasal mucosa slightly pale, no polyps. Eardrums: no redness, landmarks visualized. Good dentition; no postnasal mucus noted

Neck: No thyromegaly or lymphadenopathy noted

Heart: Regular rate and rhythm; no murmurs, rubs, or gallops

Lungs: No cough or secretions noted; slight expiratory wheezes; no other adventitious sounds

Abdominal: No masses, tenderness noted; no hepatosplenomegaly

Genitourinary: Not indicated; urine chlamydia ordered

Extremities: Normal gait

Neurological: Speech is clear but slow; thought processes appropriate; cranial nerves 2 to 12 intact

After reviewing the case and the Grading Criteria in Appendix A, jot down your notes or preliminary answers in the spaces provided below. When you are ready to submit your answers for grading (if you are working with an instructor) and reflective feedback to help you evaluate your answers, go to http://www.evolve.elsevier.com/Cappiello/ to complete this case.

Learning Issues

Before identifying your recommended Assessment and Plan, identify any learning issues that you believe are important for you to explore about this case:

Assessment

Please indicate the problems or issues you have identified that will guide your care (preferably in list form):

Plan

Please list your plans for addressing each of the problems or issues in your assessment:

Case 36

Irene Anderson
Age 39 years

Opening Scenario

Irene Anderson is a 39-year-old female here for an annual gynecological visit. She was last seen in your office one year ago. This is her second visit with you.

History of Present Illness

"Last year I saw you for my Pap smear. I have been thinking about that visit ever since. I lied to you. You asked if anyone was hurting me and I said no. *[Client is now very distraught and can barely talk.]* This is the second time that I have had an abusive partner. I'm so embarrassed. I have never told this to anyone. Everyone thinks we are a great couple. I work in town at the Pelican Coffee Shop, and I would never want all the townspeople to know this about me. He has hit me a few times, but lately he's constantly yelling and swearing at me. He makes me feel terrible all the time, like I'm no good."

Medical History

Ms. Anderson is a G2P1010, LMP two weeks ago. The visit one year ago addressed her expressed need for contraception, but she did not follow through with the plan to use depomedroxyprogesterone acetate (DMPA). She currently uses withdrawal as birth control and reports having one sexual partner in three years. She had dental surgery just before the visit last year and was using Percocet occasionally. Other surgery: Bilateral reduction mammoplasty at age 20. Reports no chronic medical problems. States that all past Pap tests were normal, and the last one was one year ago at this office. All childhood immunizations; tetanus-diphtheria (Td) five years ago; no hepatitis vaccines.

Family Medical History

MGM: 79 years old (arthritis)
MGF: Died at age 72 (myocardial infarction)

PGM: 83 years old (adult-onset DM diagnosed last year)
PGF: Died at age 56 (auto accident)
Mother: 60 years old (A&W)
Father: 62 years old (hypertension)

Social History

Has never smoked. When asked, states she is drinking alcohol to block out her concerns about the relationship. Drinks four to five drinks (beer, wine, or mixed drinks) per day. Ms. Anderson denies recreational or prescription drug use. Drinks two cups of coffee per day, no soda or tea. States she eats three balanced meals per day. Uses Stairmaster three times per week plus active job as a waitress. Sleeps five to six hours per night. Wears seatbelts.

She states it was difficult to get time off for this appointment. Works long hours and cannot miss work. Does not have health insurance. Requests that the office not call her house for any reason because her partner would become suspicious. Has lived with this partner for 1½ years. States she does not make enough to handle the rent for living alone. No children in the household. Her family lives two hours away, but is not supportive emotionally nor financially.

Medications

None

Allergies

NKDA

Review of Systems

General: No fatigue, fever, or night sweats
Integumentary: No rashes or changes in skin moles
HEENT: States chronic gum problems for which she is seeing a dentist; no problems with vision or hearing
Cardiovascular: No chest pain, heart palpitations, or syncope
Respiratory: No shortness of breath, wheezing, or coughing
Breast: No masses, pain, nipple discharge, or skin changes
Gastrointestinal: Appetite fair; no nausea, abdominal pain, constipation, diarrhea, or rectal bleeding
Genitourinary: Reports mild premenstrual symptoms; no abnormal bleeding, vaginal discharge/itching, pelvic pain, pain with intercourse, or urinary symptoms
Musculoskeletal: No pain, swelling, or injury
Neurological: Tension headaches about once a week relieved by acetaminophen; no weakness, seizures, paresthesia, or memory changes

Psychiatric: Does feel sad and anxious about life stressors at times; not feeling hopeless or suicidal

Endocrine: No weight gain, weight loss, alopecia, cold/heat intolerance, or excessive hunger/thirst

Physical Examination

Vital signs: Temperature 98.0° F; pulse 74 bpm; respirations 16/min; BP 140/90 mm Hg

Height: 5 ft 3 in; *Weight:* 110 lb

General: Well-nourished female, looks distressed

Skin: No bruising, cuts, or abrasions noted; multiple small brown nevi on trunk

HEENT: Pupils equal and reactive to light; tympanic membranes: crisp cone of light, no redness; nares patent; gums reddened; pharynx: no redness or exudate

Neck: Thyroid: no enlargement or nodularity noted; no supraclavicular lymphadenopathy

Heart: Regular rate and rhythm; no murmurs or extra sounds

Respiratory: Lungs clear to auscultation

Breasts: Faint scar lines visible on each breast secondary to reduction mammoplasty; no masses, skin changes, nipple inversion, or lymphadenopathy

Abdomen: Soft, nontender, no masses palpated; no hepatosplenomegaly

Pelvic: Vulva: no lesions or discoloration. Vagina: scant clear mucus. Cervix: no redness or lesions. Uterus: anteverted, small, nontender. Adnexa: no tenderness or enlargement

Extremities: No edema or varicosities

Neurological: Alert with appropriate affect; muscle strength testing normal (5/5); biceps, triceps, patellar, ankle reflexes 2+

After reviewing the case and the Grading Criteria in Appendix A, jot down your notes or preliminary answers in the spaces provided below. When you are ready to submit your answers for grading (if you are working with an instructor) and reflective feedback to help you evaluate your answers, go to http://www.evolve.elsevier.com/Cappiello/ to complete this case.

Learning Issues

Before identifying your recommended Assessment and Plan, identify any learning issues that you believe are important for you to explore about this case:

Assessment

Please indicate the problems or issues you have identified that will guide your care (preferably in list form):

Plan

Please list your plans for addressing each of the problems or issues in your assessment:

Case 37

Donna Downing
Age 45 years

Opening Scenario

You find a mammogram report on your desktop of a patient you saw two weeks ago. The mammogram was performed yesterday (Box 37-1). You review her health record from her visit of two weeks ago (see note).

BOX 37-1	Mammography Report for Donna Downing

DOWNING, DONNA
DIGITAL BILATERAL SCREENING MAMMOGRAM WITH R2 COMPUTER-AIDED DETECTION.
INDICATION: Screening
COMPARISON STUDY: None
BILATERAL BREAST FINDINGS (craniocaudal and mediolateral oblique projections of both breasts were obtained):
   The breast parenchyma is moderately dense. There are benign calcifications. There is a fairly well-circumscribed focal area of increased density in the inferior aspect of the right breast. This most likely represents asymmetrical fibroglandular tissue.
RECOMMENDATION: An ultrasound evaluation of the area is recommended.
BILATERAL BREASTS: BIRADS 0
RADIOLOGIST: Julia Xavier, MD

Note of Donna Downing's Visit Two Weeks Ago

History of Present Illness

"I'm here for my routine Pap smear. I have just moved to the area. My last examination was three years ago. Generally my health is good but I have been tired lately. I'd like to have my cholesterol checked because heart disease runs in my family."

Medical History

History of depression for two years. Currently on sertraline 100 mg daily through a mental health provider whom she sees every two to four weeks. Depression diagnosed two years ago; started on fluoxetine 20 mg, which caused insomnia, then switched to sertraline 100 mg per day about three months ago, which seems to be working well for her depression and she is sleeping better. G1P0AB1.

Menstrual History

Menarche age 12.5 years, regular 28-day cycles. Flow moderate for four to five days with mild cramping. Since IUD inserted has very light, 3-day menses; no cramping. No premenstrual syndrome.

Contraceptive History

Levonorgestrel 14 µg/day IUD for two years. Due to replace in one year. At age 19 was using condoms and had unintended pregnancy, which she terminated. Used oral contraceptives after abortion until she switched to IUD two years ago.

Family Medical History

MGM: 78 years old (diabetic for 1 year)
MGF: 79 years old (hypertension)
PGF: Deceased at age 70 (MI)
Mother: 65 years old (HTN, varicose veins that required surgery)
Father: 66 years old (A&W)
Paternal uncle: 70 years old (cancer, type unknown)
Paternal uncle: 77 years old (arthritis)

Social History

Long-term monogamous relationship with male partner. Living together. Computer programmer. One caffeine product per day. Nonsmoker. Two beers per night. Denies recreational drug use. Sleeps eight to nine hours per night. Exercises once per week, walks two miles on the weekend. States diet is high in prepared foods and "junk food" because does not take the time to prepare meals.

Medications

Sertraline 100 mg daily
Multivitamin daily
Metamucil daily

Allergies

Cats; NKDA

Review of Systems

General: States she feels healthy overall

HEENT: Denies history of sinus pain or problems; no current nasal problems or rhinitis; no ear or dental problems

Cardiovascular: No chest pain, palpitations

Respiratory: No shortness of breath, dyspnea

Breast: No masses or pain; performs breast self-examination every few months

Gastrointestinal: Denies heartburn, nausea and vomiting, abdominal pain, rectal bleeding; has had problems with constipation for many years; uses Metamucil daily, which controls symptoms

Genitourinary: Menarche age 12.5; LMP 1 week ago; regular 28-day cycles; denies cramping, intermenstrual bleeding, or premenstrual syndrome

Musculoskeletal: No history of fracture, sprains, joint pain

Endocrine: Fatigue over the past six months; sleeping eight to nine hours per night, no dryness of skin or hair; temperature tolerances good; weight stable

Neurological: Headaches rarely

Physical Examination

Vital signs: Temperature 98.4° F; pulse 70 bpm; respirations 16/min; BP 126/72 mm Hg

Height: 5 ft 7 in; *weight:* 175 lb; *BMI:* 27

General: Healthy, alert, 45-year-old female who looks her stated age

HEENT: Pupils equal and reactive to light; extraocular movements intact; no facial pain, nasal discharge; good dentition. Ears: no cerumen, crisp cone of light. Pharynx: no redness or exudate

Neck: No thyromegaly or supraclavicular lymphadenopathy

Heart: Regular rate and rhythm; no murmurs, rubs, or gallops

Lungs: Clear to auscultation

Breasts: No tenderness, skin changes, or masses; no palpable axillary nodes

Abdominal: Soft, no tenderness; no hepatosplenomegaly

Genitourinary: Vulva: no redness, lesions. Vagina: scant, clear discharge. Cervix: no lesions, IUD strings visible. Uterus: anteverted, anteflexed, nontender. Adnexa: no enlargement, no tenderness

Neurological: Cranial nerves 2 to 12 intact

Note from two days after visit: TSH, CBC, and Lipid Profile WNL. Advised to follow up in four weeks to discuss fatigue issue after nutrition consultation.

Note from one week after visit: Pap results WNL with negative HPV. Follow-up in five years.

After reviewing the case and the Grading Criteria in Appendix A, jot down your notes or preliminary answers in the spaces provided below. When you are ready to submit your answers for grading (if you are working with an instructor) and reflective feedback to help you evaluate your answers, go to http://www.evolve.elsevier.com/Cappiello/ to complete this case.

Learning Issues

Before identifying your recommended Assessment and Plan, identify any learning issues that you believe are important for you to explore about this case:

Assessment

Please indicate the problems or issues you have identified that will guide your care (preferably in list form):

Plan

Please list your plans for addressing each of the problems or issues in your assessment:

Case 38

1:00 PM

Emma Thurlow
Age 68 years

Opening Scenario

Emma Thurlow is a 68-year-old female who vacations in this area. She called ahead and was assured by the office staff that you would see her and take care of her allergy shots for the summer. The physician assistant who works with you gave her the shots last week. She came in with a letter and instructions from her allergist. These instructions give a gradually increasing dosage of her allergy solutions.

Part I

Today she is to get 0.5 mL subcutaneously for dust mites and molds and 0.5 mL for cats. How will you proceed? Take a few minutes to consider this before you go on to Part II. You may want to review the Case Feedback for Part I before going on to Part II.

Part II

About 15 minutes after the injections, Ms. Thurlow comes to the desk and says that her neck feels itchy. What, if anything, will you do at this point?

Part III

About 25 minutes after the injections, Ms. Thurlow says that she is having a hard time breathing. You examine her and find that she is red over most of her torso. You listen to her lungs and hear significant inspiratory and expiratory wheezes. How will you proceed?

After reviewing the case and the Grading Criteria in Appendix A, jot down your notes or preliminary answers in the spaces provided below. When you are ready to submit your answers for grading (if you are working with an instructor) and reflective feedback to help you evaluate your answers, go to **http://www.evolve.elsevier.com/Cappiello/** to complete this case.

Learning Issues

Before identifying your recommended Assessment and Plan, identify any learning issues that you believe are important for you to explore about this case:

Assessment

Please indicate the problems or issues you have identified that will guide your care (preferably in list form):

Plan

Please list your plans for addressing each of the problems or issues in your assessment:

Case 39

Albert Steinberg
Age 44 years

Opening Scenario

Albert Steinberg is a 44-year-old male on your schedule for a cough and fever.

History of Present Illness

"I have been sick for about a week. I've felt like I have been running a low-grade fever, but when I took my temperature two days ago, it was just a little over 100° F. I have been coughing up some reddish brown sputum, but not all that much of it. I cough fairly frequently, but I didn't have any cough medicine in the house. I really hope that you can do something for me because I haven't been this sick in a long time. I feel like I've been run over by a truck. I've had bronchitis a couple of times before, but it's never been this bad. I had a tuberculosis test four or five years ago and it was negative." Mr. Steinberg has no known exposures, although he is exposed to a lot of people through his police work. He denies sweats and chills. His appetite is decreased but still "okay." He denies shortness of breath but does note that he gets winded much more quickly lately. His wife had some Sudafed from the last time she was sick, and she wanted him to try that, so he has been taking it for about three days.

Medical History

Tonsillectomy and adenoidectomy as a child. Denies other surgeries or hospitalizations. No history of DM, cancer, or heart disease.

Family Medical History

MGM: Deceased at age 82 (breast cancer)
MGF: Deceased at age 77 (heart attack)
PGM: Deceased at age 80 (complications of type 2 DM)
PGF: Deceased at age 74 (stroke)
Mother: 81 years old (A&W)

Father: Deceased at age 80 (stroke)
Son: 22 years old (A&W)

Social History

Police sergeant. Married. Wife works as an office manager for an oil company. One grown son who lives on his own. Smokes 1½ packs per day since age 20. A few drinks on the weekend; never more than two to three beers in an evening; goes all week without alcohol.

Medications

Vitamin C, 2000 mg per day
Pseudoephedrine Long Acting (12 hour), 120 mg bid for the past three days

Allergies

NKDA

Review of Systems

General: Good energy level usually; feels energy is lower and stamina is less than usual
Integumenatary: No itching or rashes
HEENT: No history of head injury; no corrective lenses; denies eye pain, excessive tearing, blurring, or change in vision; no tinnitus or vertigo; denies frequent colds, hay fever, or sinus problems
Neck: No lumps, goiters, or pain
Respiratory: Denies shortness of breath (usually) with normal activity; no recent nocturnal dyspnea, mild shortness of breath with heavy activity
Cardiovascular: No chest pain; no excessive bruising; no history of transfusions
Gastrointestinal: No nausea, vomiting, constipation, or diarrhea; denies belching, bloating, and black or clay-colored stools
Genitourinary: No dysuria; no difficulty starting stream
Musculoskeletal: Mild joint pain with significant activity
Neurological: No headaches, seizures
Endocrine: No polyuria, polyphagia, polydipsia; temperature tolerances good

Physical Examination

Vital signs: Temperature 98.4° F; pulse 86 bpm; respirations 22/min; BP 126/82 mm Hg
Height: 5 ft 10 in; *weight:* 172 lb; *BMI:* 24.7
General: Well developed, well nourished; in no acute distress; appears stated age

HEENT: Normocephalic without masses or lesions; pupils equal, round, and reactive to light; extraocular movements intact; fundi benign, nares patent and noninjected; throat without redness or lesions

Neck: Supple without thyromegaly or adenopathy

Respiratory: Coarse crackles scattered throughout both lungs; no wheezes; symmetrical resonant percussion notes; lung sounds do not change with cough

Heart: Regular rate and rhythm; no murmurs, rubs, or gallops

Abdominal: No hepatosplenomegaly; abdomen soft, nontender; bowel sounds normoactive

Genitourinary: Normal male, circumcised, both testicles descended

Extremities: Range of motion functionally intact; no cyanosis, clubbing, or edema

Neurological: Reflexes 2+ at Achilles, patellar, biceps, triceps, and brachioradialis; no Babinski signs present

After reviewing the case and the Grading Criteria in Appendix A, jot down your notes or preliminary answers in the spaces provided below. When you are ready to submit your answers for grading (if you are working with an instructor) and reflective feedback to help you evaluate your answers, go to **http://www.evolve.elsevier.com/Cappiello/** to complete this case.

Learning Issues

Before identifying your recommended Assessment and Plan, identify any learning issues that you believe are important for you to explore about this case:

Continued

Assessment

Please indicate the problems or issues you have identified that will guide your care (preferably in list form):

Plan

Please list your plans for addressing each of the problems or issues in your assessment:

1:30 PM

Betty Hackett
Age 33 years

Opening Scenario

Betty Hackett is a 33-year-old pregnant woman on your schedule for a 20-week pre-natal check. You have her initial database (see note) and her pregnancy flow chart (Table 40-1). Her laboratory workup is documented in the flow chart.

Betty Hackett's Health Record from 12 Weeks Ago (First Prenatal Visit)

Medical History

Ms. Hackett is a 33-year-old female who is new to this practice. She is about four weeks late for her period and has tested positive for pregnancy on a home pregnancy test. This pregnancy is planned and wanted. She and her husband have been trying to conceive for about one year. Pregnancy history: One medication abortion at seven weeks when she was age 19. No other pregnancies. On oral contraceptives (OCs) until about one year ago.

Family Medical History

Genetic history: No known familial disorders, including cystic fibrosis, musculoskeletal disorders, hematological disorders, or chromosomal abnormalities.

MGM: 82 years old (mild arthritis)
MGF: Deceased at age 71 (heart attack)
PGM: Deceased at age 64 (Alzheimer's disease)
PGF: Deceased at age 79 (stroke)
Mother: 63 years old (breast cancer at age 58, A&W following radiation and chemo-therapy)
Father: 65 years old (glaucoma)
Brother: Deceased at age 12 (leukemia)

TABLE 40-1   Pregnancy Flow Chart for Betty Hackett

Type of Data	WEEK OF PREGNANCY			
	8	12	16	20
BP (mm Hg)	106/64	110/74	116/80	118/82
Urine protein	Negative	Negative	Negative	Trace
Urine sugar	Negative	Negative	Negative	Negative
Height	5 ft 3 in			
Weight (lb)	127	126	128	132
Fundal height	@sp	3 fb↑sp @umb		
Movement				
Blood type	B+			
FHR	160	144	144	
Pelvic examination				
NIPT	Negative			
AFP	15.4			
Hematocrit	37%			
US				
GC/chlamydia	Negative			
RPR	Negative			
HBsAg	Negative			

EDB (dates) _____
EDB (US) _____
LMP: 20 weeks ago
Notes:
8 weeks: Morning sickness about the same; conservative management seems to be working
12 weeks: Morning sickness still improving but not totally gone; NIPT ordered
16 weeks: AFP ordered; morning sickness only occasionally now
18½ weeks: Laboratory report back; AFP 15.4 (not elevated)

Social History

Married for 10 years. Works as a bank loan officer. Never smoked. Alcohol: Very rare glass of wine. No pets. They own their own home and state that finances are not a big issue for them.

Medications

Daily multivitamin containing 400 µg of folic acid

Allergies

NKDA

Review of Systems

General: Good energy level

Integumentary: No itching, rashes, or other lesions

HEENT: No history of head injury; no corrective lenses; denies eye pain, excessive tearing, blurring, or change in vision; no tinnitus or vertigo; denies frequent colds, hay fever, or sinus problems; occasional headaches since pregnancy began

Neck: No lumps, goiters, or pain

Thorax: Denies shortness of breath or paroxysmal nocturnal dyspnea

Breast: No breast pain or discharge

Cardiovascular: No chest pain; no shortness of breath with normal activity. No excessive bruising; no history of transfusions.

Gastrointestinal: Mild nausea, rare vomiting, no constipation or diarrhea; denies belching, bloating, and black or clay-colored stools

Genitourinary: No difficulty starting stream; denies dysuria but notes frequency; no vaginal discharge or bleeding since last period

Musculoskeletal: No joint pains or swelling

Neurological: No seizures

Endocrine: No polyuria, polyphagia, polydipsia; temperature tolerances good

Physical Examination

Vital signs: Temperature 98.4° F; pulse 78 bpm; respirations 18/min; BP 106/64 mm Hg

Height: 5 ft 3 in; *weight:* 127 lb

General: Well developed, well nourished; in no acute distress; appears stated age; denies history of physical abuse; feels safe in current relationship

Diet: No red meat; drinks 1.5 liters of Diet Coke per day; otherwise uses food pyramid approach

HEENT: Normocephalic without masses or lesions; pupils equal, round, and reactive to light; extraocular movements intact; fundi benign; nares patent and non-infected; throat without redness or lesions

Neck: Supple without thyromegaly or adenopathy

Thorax: Clear to auscultation and percussion

Breast: No asymmetry, masses, or discharge

Heart: Regular rate and rhythm; no murmurs, rubs, or gallops

Abdominal: No hepatosplenomegaly; abdomen soft, nontender; bowel sounds normoactive; rectum without masses or hemorrhoids; stool brown; guaiac negative

Genitourinary: External without lesions; vaginal mucosa pink; cervix without visible lesions; no discharge noted; uterus anteroflexed and slightly enlarged; no adnexal tenderness

Extremities: Range of motion functionally intact; no cyanosis, clubbing, or edema

Neurological: Reflexes 2+ at Achilles, patellar, biceps, triceps, and brachioradialis; no Babinski signs present; cranial nerves 2 through 12 intact

Today's Visit

You are seeing Ms. Hackett today for her 20-week visit. Please indicate what you will do in today's visit. Note that the BP, weight, and urine dip have been performed by your office staff.

As you are closing the interview, when you ask if she has any other questions or concerns, she responds that she has been talking with her husband about the issue of circumcision if they have a boy. She says they are not sure about what to do and wants to discuss this topic with you. How will you approach the discussion?

She also asks if, or when, she will have to stop sexual activity. How will you respond?

After reviewing the case and the Grading Criteria in Appendix A, jot down your notes or preliminary answers in the spaces provided below. When you are ready to submit your answers for grading (if you are working with an instructor) and reflective feedback to help you evaluate your answers, go to http://www.evolve.elsevier.com/Cappiello/ to complete this case.

Learning Issues

Before identifying your recommended Assessment and Plan, identify any learning issues that you believe are important for you to explore about this case:

Assessment

Please indicate the problems or issues you have identified that will guide your care (preferably in list form):

Plan

Please list your plans for addressing each of the problems or issues in your assessment:

1:45 PM

Olga Manjakhina
Age 54 years

Opening Scenario

Olga Manjakhina is a 54-year-old woman of Russian heritage on your schedule for urinary incontinence (UI). She has not been to your practice before.

History of Present Illness

"I have been having problems over the past three to four months with losing my urine. For quite some time, I have leaked a small amount of urine when I laugh or when I sneeze, but over the past few months it seems to be getting worse. There are also times more recently, for about the past month, when I am just sitting quietly and I get an uncontrollable urge to urinate. When I urinate at that time it is in fairly large amounts. I have been using incontinence pads with good success in keeping my clothing dry." Patient denies dysuria and difficulty starting stream. She loses her urine whenever she coughs and, at times, when she is lifting or carrying things, or even at rest as noted. No known history of urinary tract infections (UTIs). Up once each night to void. Voids about every 1½ hours during the day in moderate amounts.

Medical History

She has been quite healthy all of her life. The delivery of one of her children was "traumatic." The doctor had a hard time delivering the baby and had to use forceps; she describes it as very painful. "The doctors thought he might die, but he did fine." Menopause at age 49.

Family Medical History

Mother: 84 years old (mild arthritis)
Father: 86 years old (mild lung problems)
Four sisters: Range from ages 40 to 61 years (A&W)
Two brothers: ages 52 and 57 (A&W)
Two children: ages 30 and 34 (A&W)

Social History

Lives with husband who is an engineer. Came to the United States with family from Leningrad, Russia (now St. Petersburg), 14 years ago. Smokes one pack per day. One alcoholic drink per evening. Does not work outside of the home. Limits her social activities to about two hours because of urine leakage.

Medications

None

Allergies

NKDA

Review of Systems

General: Good energy level
Integumentary: No itching or rashes
HEENT: No history of head injury or headaches; no corrective lenses; denies eye pain; no excessive tearing, blurring, or change in vision; no tinnitus or vertigo; denies frequent colds, hay fever, or sinus problems
Neck: No lumps, goiters, or pain
Respiratory: Denies shortness of breath with normal activity, paroxysmal nocturnal dyspnea
Cardiovascular: No chest pain, no excessive bruising, no history of transfusions
Gastrointestinal: No nausea, vomiting, constipation, or diarrhea; denies belching, bloating, and black or clay-colored stools
Genitourinary: See History of Present Illness
Musculoskeletal: No joint pain or swelling
Neurological: No seizures; denies numbness, paresthesias, or weakness
Endocrine: No polyuria, polyphagia, polydipsia; temperature tolerances good

Physical Examination

Vital signs: Temperature 98° F; pulse 76 bpm; respirations 18/min; BP120/74 mm Hg
Height: 5 ft 6 in; *weight:* 167 lb; *BMI:* 27.0
General: Well developed, well nourished; in no acute distress; appears stated age
HEENT: Normocephalic without masses or lesions; pupils equal, round, and reactive to light; extraocular movements intact; fundi benign; nares patent and noninjected; throat without redness or lesions
Neck: Supple without thyromegaly or adenopathy

Chest: Clear to auscultation and percussion

Heart: Regular rate and rhythm; no murmurs, rubs, or gallops

Abdominal: No hepatosplenomegaly; abdomen soft, nontender; bowel sounds normo-active; rectal without masses; stool brown; guaiac negative; normal sphincter tone

Genitourinary: External without lesions; vaginal mucosa pink with mild atrophy; cervix without gross lesions; no discharge noted; uterus is anteroflexed; no adnexal tenderness; Grade 1 cystocele; no rectocele

Extremities: Range of motion functionally intact; no cyanosis, clubbing, or edema

Neurological: Reflexes 2+ at Achilles, patellar, biceps, triceps, and brachioradialis; no Babinski signs present

Laboratory tests: Pap smear sent. Dip urine: SG 1.010, negative for glucose and protein, positive for nitrites and leukocytes

After reviewing the case and the Grading Criteria in Appendix A, jot down your notes or preliminary answers in the spaces provided below. When you are ready to submit your answers for grading (if you are working with an instructor) and reflective feedback to help you evaluate your answers, go to **http://www.evolve.elsevier.com/Cappiello/** to complete this case.

Learning Issues

Before identifying your recommended Assessment and Plan, identify any learning issues that you believe are important for you to explore about this case:

Assessment

Please indicate the problems or issues you have identified that will guide your care (preferably in list form):

Continued

Plan

Please list your plans for addressing each of the problems or issues in your assessment:

Case 42

Justin Baker
Age 3½ years

Opening Scenario

Justin Baker is a 3½-year-old boy in your office with red, "weepy" eyes. He was last seen for an 18-month well-child check.

History of Present Illness

(Obtained from mother)

"This happens off and on. This is probably his third episode. I haven't really noticed a pattern. The other two episodes cleared up on their own. One episode was about 3 months ago, and the other one was about this same time last year. This episode started 3 days ago. I haven't done anything for it except some warm soaks with a washcloth. He never had it this bad before, but his sister Jessie did, so I brought her in, got a cream, and it went away within a couple of days. Justin's right eye is now very red, and he feels like it has sand in it. It was just a little crusty this morning. The crust was yellowish. I just washed it off with a warm cloth. His left eye is red but less so, and it did not really have a crust on it this morning. He has had a runny nose this week as well but no other symptoms."

Medical History

Normal spontaneous vaginal delivery. Apgar scores were 10 and 10. Ear infections at 2 months, 5 months, 9 months, and 18 months. Immunization record is shown in Table 42-1. Growth percentiles are consistent in the approximately 60th percentile for height and 80th for weight. Milestones all within normal limits on previous visits. Toilet trained but occasionally wakes up wet. Sleeps about 10 hours per night but really hates to go to bed. Likes to dress himself and likes to draw.

Family Medical History

MGM: 51 years old (DM)
MGF: 53 years old (A&W)

PGM: 50 years old (A&W)
PGF: 53 years old (MI 2 years ago)
Mother: 26 years old (A&W)
Father: 26 years old (A&W)
One sister: 20 months old (A&W)

TABLE 42-1	Immunization Record for Justin Baker, 3½ Years Old		
Vaccine	Date	Initials	Notes
DTaP #1	2 mo	MDO	
DTap #2	4 mo	MDO	
DTaP #3	6 mo	MDO	
DTaP #4	15 mo	MDO	
Rotavirus #1	2 mo	MDO	
Rotavirus #2	4 mo	MDO	
IPV #1	2 mo	MDO	
IPV #2	4 mo	MDO	
IPV #3	6 mo	MDO	
MMR	15 mo	MDO	
Varicella	15 mo	MDO	
HBV #1	2 mo	MDO	
HBV #2	4 mo	MDO	
HBV #3	6 mo	MDO	
Hib #1	2 mo	MDO	
Hib #2	4 mo	MDO	
Hib #3	6 mo	MDO	
Hib #4	12 mo	MDO	
PCV13 #1	2 mo	MDO	
PCV13 #2	4 mo	MDO	
PCV13 #3	6 mo	MDO	
PCV13 #4	12 mo	MDO	
Hepatitis A	12 mo	MDO	

Social History

Lives with both parents and younger sister (who is now 20 months old). Father works as a maintenance man at local factory (makes electrical parts for lamps, etc.). Mother works part time at local video store (Mondays, Wednesdays, and Fridays). Justin attends family day care when his mother is working.

Medications

None

Allergies

NKDA

Review of Systems

(Obtained from mother)
General: Good energy level, eats well, sleeps well
Integumentary: No itching or rashes
HEENT: No history of head injury; no corrective lenses; denies frequent colds, hay fever, or sinus problems; teeth present without obvious caries, brushes teeth with parent assistance
Neck: No lumps, goiters, or pain
Thorax: Denies shortness of breath
Cardiovascular: No chest pain; no shortness of breath with normal activity. No excessive bruising; no history of transfusions.
Gastrointestinal: No nausea, vomiting, constipation, or diarrhea
Genitourinary: Toilet trained, circumcised; BM daily, without difficulty
Musculoskeletal: No joint pain or swelling
Neurological: No seizures
Endocrine: No polyuria, polyphagia, polydipsia; temperature tolerances good

Physical Examination

Vital signs: Temperature 98° F; pulse 76 bpm; respirations 18/min
Weight: 39 lb
General: Well developed, well nourished; in no acute distress; curious, friendly, follows instructions
Nutrition: Eats from all four food groups; frequent snacker and tends to like the same foods over and over again (scrambled eggs, pizza, fish sticks); drinks about 20 oz of milk per day

HEENT: Normocephalic without masses or lesions; pupils equal, round, and reactive to light; extraocular movements intact; cover/uncover test—uncovered eye maintained position, conjunctiva injected both palpebral and scleral; no ciliary flush; moderate amount of clear discharge present; nares patent and noninjected; throat without redness or lesions; tympanic membranes (TMs) noninjected; cone of light crisp; TMs mobile

Neck: Supple without thyromegaly or adenopathy

Thorax: Clear to auscultation and percussion

Heart: Regular rate and rhythm; no murmurs, rubs, or gallops

Abdominal: No hepatosplenomegaly; abdomen soft, nontender

Extremities: Full function; no cyanosis, clubbing, or edema

Neurological: Gross and fine motor intact, developmental milestones achieved—speaks three- to four-word sentences, uses pronouns and plurals; knows age, sex, and full name; asks questions

After reviewing the case and the Grading Criteria in Appendix A, jot down your notes or preliminary answers in the spaces provided below. When you are ready to submit your answers for grading (if you are working with an instructor) and reflective feedback to help you evaluate your answers, go to **http://www.evolve.elsevier.com/Cappiello/** to complete this case.

Learning Issues

Before identifying your recommended Assessment and Plan, identify any learning issues that you believe are important for you to explore about this case:

Assessment

Please indicate the problems or issues you have identified that will guide your care (preferably in list form):

Plan

Please list your plans for addressing each of the problems or issues in your assessment:

Case 43

Curt Ozana

Age 36 years

Opening Scenario

Curt Ozana is a 36-year-old male scheduled for an episodic visit. He is new to your practice.

History of Present Illness

"Yesterday I began having pain in my right scrotum. The pain has been increasing. I don't remember any trauma to the area." The patient denies urethral discharge or burning. No history of prior urinary tract infections, prostatitis, or renal calculi. New female sexual partner two months ago. Does not use condoms.

Medical History

Denies any hospitalizations or major medical problems. Outpatient vasectomy two years ago. No other surgeries.

Last physical examination was several years ago (does not remember exactly). Had all childhood immunizations, including measles-mumps-rubella (MMR) but not hepatitis A or B. Last tetanus was six years ago.

Family Medical History

Mother: 70 years old (Parkinson's disease diagnosed one year ago)
Father: 72 years old (COPD)
Sister: 40 years old (A&W)
Brother: 37 years old (A&W)

Social History

Divorced for one year. Has two children, ages 5 and 7. Works full time as a computer programmer. Nonsmoker. Drinks 10 drinks per week. Denies any drug use.

Medications

None

Allergies

Penicillin, causes hives

Review of Systems

Cardiovascular: Denies any chest pain, dyspnea
Respiratory: Denies shortness of breath, asthma, environmental allergies
Gastrointestinal: Denies hepatitis or liver problems; no abdominal or flank pain
Genitourinary: No history of undescended testicles; denies history of kidney or urinary tract problems; no recent instrumentation of urinary tract; no history of sexually transmitted infections; states a groin rash has been present for several months; he has used an over-the-counter cream when it is itchy and bothersome for a day or so, but then he forgets to use it once the itching improves; denies rashes elsewhere on body

Physical Examination

Vital signs: Temperature 98.4° F; pulse 74 bpm; respirations 16/min; BP 110/74 mm Hg
BMI: 26
General: States overall health is good
Heart: Regular rate and rhythm, no murmurs, rubs, or gallops
Lungs: Clear to auscultation
Abdominal: No tenderness, guarding, or masses palpated; no hepatosplenomegaly, costovertebral angle tenderness, or suprapubic tenderness noted; no inguinal masses or lymphadenopathy noted
Genitourinary: Right testis: red, swollen to twice the normal size, tender; raising testes decreases the pain; positive cremasteric reflex; transillumination negative; no hydrocele, spermatocele, varicocele, or epididymal cyst noted. Left testis: no redness, enlargement, or tenderness; no inguinal or femoral hernias noted. Faint, dull red rash noted in right and left groin area; scaly plaques with distinct margins covering a small portion of groin area
Lower extremities: No rashes, lesions on skin

After reviewing the case and the Grading Criteria in Appendix A, jot down your notes or preliminary answers in the spaces provided below. When you are ready to submit your answers for grading (if you are working with an instructor) and reflective feedback to help you evaluate your answers, go to **http://www.evolve.elsevier.com/Cappiello/** to complete this case.

Learning Issues

Before identifying your recommended Assessment and Plan, identify any learning issues that you believe are important for you to explore about this case:

Assessment

Please indicate the problems or issues you have identified that will guide your care (preferably in list form):

Plan

Please list your plans for addressing each of the problems or issues in your assessment:

Case 44

Melanie Roberge
Age 20 years

Opening Scenario

Melanie Roberge is a 20-year-old female scheduled for an episodic visit. She is new to your practice.

History of Present Illness

"I have a vaginal discharge that I want checked out. It is a gray, fishy-smelling discharge with no itching. The discharge has been going on for weeks. I used a cream for yeast infections from the drugstore. The cream seemed to help a little bit for the first week but the symptoms are just as annoying again. I recently moved here and although I continue to drive the 35 miles to see my provider for Suboxone, I'd like to establish care here. Can I transfer to you for my Suboxone treatment?"

Medical History

No hospitalizations or surgery. Had all childhood immunizations as a child, including the HPV series. Most recent Tdap at age 13. G1P1. Using LNG-IUD since birth of son. Last Pap smear at postpartum visit and states it was negative.

Family Medical History

MGM: 61 years old (hypercholesterolemia)
MGF: 62 years old (lung problems, heavy smoker)
PGM: 65 years old (cirrhosis, alcoholic)
PGF: Died at age 69 (colon cancer)
Mother: 41 years old (smoker)
Father: 42 years old (alcoholic)
Sister: 16 years old (A&W)

Social History

Graduated from high school and now works cleaning houses. History of substance abuse. Was in motor vehicle accident two years ago, prescribed Vicodin for pain; became addicted to opiates. When her health-care provider would no longer provide Vicodin, she turned to buying it on the street and reportedly started snorting heroin because it was easier to obtain. When she became pregnant, she entered Suboxone treatment and has stayed on it since. Drinks one or two beers, 2 to 3 times a week. Nonsmoker. Lives with her one-year-old son and his father on and off (her son's father has a drug problem).

Medications

Buprenorphine/naloxone (Suboxone)

Allergies

NKDA

Review of Symptoms

General: Appetite fair; no weight changes; denies fever, chills, night sweats; sleeps six hours per night and fatigued during the day
HEENT: No history of frequent colds, sinusitis, rhinitis, environmental allergies, ear infections; hearing and vision normal; no dental problems, last saw a dentist one year ago
Cardiovascular: No chest pain, palpitations
Respiratory: No history of wheezing, asthma, shortness of breath, dyspnea
Gastrointestinal: No heartburn, nausea, vomiting, diarrhea; frequent constipation, no hemorrhoids; lower abdominal pain for two weeks
Genitourinary: G1P1; menarche at age 13; usually no menses with IUD but occasionally has a few days of spotting at time of menses, no cramping, last menstrual period three weeks ago with two days of very light spotting; sexually active, one male partner; she does not know if he has other partners; they do not use condoms
Musculoskeletal: No history of fractures or sprains; occasional myalgias; no joint pain
Endocrine: Temperature tolerances good; no skin or hair changes; occasional fatigue
Neurological: Occasional headaches relieved by ibuprofen; no weakness, seizures; denies depression or history of psychiatric illness; denies current history of feeling sad, powerless

Physical Examination

Vital signs: Temperature 98.6° F; pulse 74 bpm; respirations 20/min; BP 130/76 mm Hg

Height: 5 ft 1 in; *weight:* 135 lb; *BMI:* 26

General: Healthy appearing, slightly overweight young female; oriented to time and place

Skin: Without lesions, bruising

Abdominal: Abdomen soft, no tenderness or masses; no hepatosplenomegaly

Genitourinary: Vulva: no lesions, redness. Vagina: moderate amount of gray discharge. Cervix: no lesions, negative cervical motion tenderness, IUD strings visible. Adnexa: nontender, no enlargement bilaterally

After reviewing the case and the Grading Criteria in Appendix A, jot down your notes or preliminary answers in the spaces provided below. When you are ready to submit your answers for grading (if you are working with an instructor) and reflective feedback to help you evaluate your answers, go to **http://www.evolve.elsevier.com/Cappiello/** to complete this case.

Learning Issues

Before identifying your recommended Assessment and Plan, identify any learning issues that you believe are important for you to explore about this case:

Assessment

Please indicate the problems or issues you have identified that will guide your care (preferably in list form):

Continued

Plan

Please list your plans for addressing each of the problems or issues in your assessment:

Case 45

Renée Jones
Age 35 years

Opening Scenario

Renée Jones is a 35-year-old female with a complaint of wrist pain near the base of her right thumb. This is her first visit to your office. Her provider over the past several years has been her certified nurse midwife (CNM). She is 16 weeks postpartum.

History of Present Illness

"About two weeks ago, I began to notice pain near the base of my right thumb. It is worse at the end of the day and after use. The pain is sharp at times but more often 'achy' as the day goes on. Ice seems to ease the discomfort. Two acetaminophen have decreased the pain, but I am hesitant to use a large amount of any medication while nursing, even acetaminophen. I take a dose every one to two days. I am a physical therapist and do a lot of writing and massaging in my work. I returned to work four weeks ago after a 12-week maternity leave. Other activities that aggravate my wrist include holding the baby while nursing, and the usual household activities of cleaning and laundry. Currently, I have no hobbies or specific exercise workout regimen other than walking."

She is right hand dominant. She has noticed a decreased range of motion of her right thumb, difficulty gripping, and catching and locking at the base of her thumb.

Medical History

No surgeries. Three hospitalizations, each for childbirth. Negative history of any major medical problems, including arthritis. Had all usual childhood immunizations, including hepatitis A and B. Was immunized in pregnancy with inactivated influenza vaccine and Tdap, as recommended.

Family Medical History

Parents: (A&W)
One sibling: 30 years old (A&W)
Three children: Newborn, 5-year-old, and 8-year-old (A&W)

Social History

Married with three children. Nonsmoker. Alcohol rarely used, especially since pregnant and nursing. Sleep interrupted, nurses infant twice per night. States that infant is gaining weight and thriving.

Medications

Prenatal vitamins daily
Tylenol: 2 tablets every 1 to 2 days

Allergies

NKDA

Review of Systems

General: Feels her health is excellent
Genitourinary: No menses since delivery; lactating; uses diaphragm faithfully; had Pap smear, which was negative at 6-week postpartum check
Musculoskeletal: No history of joint pain, arthralgias, myalgias; no history of sprains, fractures, or trauma; denies neck, shoulder, or elbow pain or injuries; low back discomfort during pregnancy, which resolved postpartum; aware of, and uses, appropriate body mechanics in her job

Physical Examination

Vital signs: Temperature 97.8° F; pulse 90 bpm; respirations 22/min; BP 118/70 mm Hg
Height: 5 ft 7 in; *weight:* 172 lb; *BMI:* 27
Neck: Full active range of motion (AROM) without discomfort, no tenderness to palpation
Shoulder: Right: Full AROM without discomfort, no tenderness to palpation
Elbow: Right: Full AROM without discomfort, no tenderness to palpation
Wrist/hand: No redness, thenar atrophy, or dry skin; very mild soft tissue swelling; palpation reveals tenderness on the radial and ulnar borders of the anatomical snuff box; no tenderness on the floor of the snuff box; pain with resisted movement of thumb and first extensor; ROM of thumb limited in the extremes by pain;

some decrease in thumb abduction; strength and grip slightly less with right hand because of pain; mild crepitus with radial/ulnar movement; no neurosensory, neurovascular changes; full ROM of the wrist; Finkelstein test positive; Phalen's test negative; Tinel sign negative

After reviewing the case and the Grading Criteria in Appendix A, jot down your notes or preliminary answers in the spaces provided below. When you are ready to submit your answers for grading (if you are working with an instructor) and reflective feedback to help you evaluate your answers, go to **http://www.evolve.elsevier.com/Cappiello/** to complete this case.

Learning Issues

Before identifying your recommended Assessment and Plan, identify any learning issues that you believe are important for you to explore about this case:

Assessment

Please indicate the problems or issues you have identified that will guide your care (preferably in list form):

Plan

Please list your plans for addressing each of the problems or issues in your assessment:

3:30 PM

Judy Marland
Age 81 years

Opening Scenario

Judy Marland is an 81-year-old female in your office for memory problems. She is accompanied by her daughter who lives three miles away. Her daughter tells you that she wanted somebody to look at her mother because she feels her mother has been getting a lot more forgetful. She forgot to pay the phone bill for two months and the phone company was threatening to shut off her phone. The daughter states that she did not notice any sudden change; it just seems to have come on gradually. You have 30 minutes scheduled to obtain a history, do a physical examination, and review laboratory work that was done two months ago when Ms. Marland had cataract surgery. She is doing well postsurgery and says that her vision has improved significantly.

History of Present Illness

"I have problems remembering sometimes, but who doesn't?" Based on history from her daughter, this 81-year-old woman has been becoming progressively more confused over the past two months. At times, she is unable to find rooms in her own home and has forgotten to pay bills. Ms. Marland's history is limited by her memory and her daughter's lack of knowledge of events in the remote past.

Medical History

Hysterectomy about 20 years ago. G3P2102. Cataract surgery 2 months ago as noted after the hysterectomy. Had been followed by Dr. Breene, who left the area about one year ago. Your practice assumed the care of Dr. Breene's patients, but no record can be found on Ms. Marland. *[Instead, state something like: Thus, you do not have documentation for diagnoses and associated medications.]*

Ms. Marland's complete blood count (CBC) (Table 46-1), chemistry profile (Table 46-2), urinalysis (Table 46-3), and chest x-ray (CXR) examination (Box 46-1) from cataract surgery two months ago are provided.

TABLE 46-1 Complete Blood Count (CBC) for Judy Marland from 2 Months Ago

CBC	Result	Normal Range
WBC	4.6	4.5–10.8
RBC	3.45 L	4.20–5.40
Hgb	10.1 L	12.0–16.0
Hct	33.2 L	37.0–47.0
MCV	78.3 L	81.0–99.0
MCH	28.2	27.0–32.0
MCHC	32.4	32.0–36.0
RDW	16.2 H	11.0–16.0
Platelets	221	150–450
Segs	66 H	50–65
Lymphocytes	21 L	25–45
Monocytes	8	0–10
Eosinophils	5 H	0–4

TABLE 46-2 Chemistry Profile for Judy Marland from 2 Months Ago

Test	Result	Normal
FBS	130 H	60–100
BUN	27	8–28
Creatinine	1.0	0.5–1.5
Sodium	128 L	135–145
Potassium	5.3	3.5–5.5
Chloride	104	95–105
Albumin	3.7 L	4.0–6.0
Total protein	6.3 L	6.5–8.0
Alkaline phosphate	100	30–120
ALT	22	0–40
AST	28	0–40
LDH	134	50–150
Cholesterol	252 H	110–200
Calcium	8.6 L	8.8–10.2
GGT	29	0–30
Magnesium	2.1	1.6–2.4
Bilirubin	0.7	0.1–1.0
Conjugated bilirubin	0.1	0.0–0.2
Iron	17 L	60–160
Uric acid	6.3	2.0–7.0

TABLE 46-3 Urinalysis for Judy Marland from 2 Months Ago

Color	Yellow
Character	Clear
SG	1.025
pH	5.0
Glucose	Negative
Nitrite	Negative
WBCs	0–2
RBCs	0–1
Epithelial cells	0–5
Crystals	None

BOX 46-1 Chest X-ray Examination for Judy Marland from 2 Months Ago

The lung fields are clear of infiltrates. The pulmonary vasculature and markings are normal. The heart size is in the upper range of normal limits.

Impression: Normal chest x-ray examination.

Boyd Bates, DO

Family Medical History

Mother: Died at age 54 (breast cancer; had type 2 diabetes mellitus [DM])
Father: Died at age 77 (stroke; also had type 2 DM)
Three children: One son died 30 years ago (automobile accident); daughter, age 58
    (A&W); son, age 54 (high cholesterol)

Social History

Does not smoke or drink alcohol. She is a retired seamstress. Husband died 10+ years
ago from MI at age 74. Neighbor visits her at her home twice per week. She has one
son who lives about 1000 miles away. Daughter lives three miles away and takes her
to church on Sundays. Daughter is a school teacher, and son-in-law is an attorney.

Medications

Triamterene/hydrochlorothiazide (Dyazide), 1 tablet orally (PO) daily
Aspirin, 81 mg PO daily
Benadryl, 25 mg at bedtime
Tums, two tablets three times a day
Multivitamin, one tablet PO daily

Allergies

NKDA

Review of Systems

General: Denies weight loss or gain, fatigue, fever or chills, trouble sleeping, night
    sweats
HEENT: Denies diplopia, blurring, hearing impairment, sore throats
Cardiovascular: Denies chest pain, shortness of breath, dyspnea on exertion, paroxys-
    mal nocturnal dyspnea, or peripheral swelling; denies excessive bruising
Respiratory: No shortness of breath, dyspnea on exertion, cough
Gastrointestinal: Denies anorexia, nausea, vomiting, constipation, diarrhea, black or
    clay-colored stools
Neurological Denies headaches, history of head trauma; no vertigo, balance is normal
    subjectively; denies weakness, numbness, seizures, depression, excessive stress,
    and anxiety
Genitourinary: Denies dysuria, hematuria
Musculoskeletal: Denies joint or back pain

Physical Examination

Vital signs: Temperature 96.6° F; pulse 88 bpm; respirations 24/min; BP 108/44 mm Hg

Height: 5 ft 3 in; *weight:* 112 lb; *BMI:* 19.8

Skin: Slightly pale without open areas

HEENT: Head is normocephalic, atraumatic; pupils equal, round, and reactive to light; extraocular movements intact; Snellen 20/40 using both eyes with glasses; tympanic membranes noninjected without excessive cerumen; whisper test 2/3 bilaterally; nares are patent without redness or exudate; throat is noninjected; tongue is midline; palate rises symmetrically; edentulous with well-fitting dentures

Neck: Supple without thyromegaly, adenopathy, or carotid bruits

Heart: Regular rate and rhythm; no rubs or gallops; grade III/VI murmur heard at the fourth ICS LSB; peripheral pulses are 1+ at popliteal, dorsalis pedis, and posterior tibial; pulses 2+ at femoral, radial, and carotid

Lungs: Clear to auscultation and percussion except for fine bibasilar crackles, which clear with coughing

Breasts: Without masses or discharge

Abdominal: Soft, nontender; no hepatosplenomegaly; rectal is with brown stool, no masses; stool is guaiac negative

Genitourinary: Genitalia without external lesions or rashes; pelvic examination not done

Extremities: Without cyanosis, clubbing, or edema; reflexes are 2+ at the biceps, triceps, brachioradialis, patellar, and Achilles; no Babinski signs present; strength and sensation in upper and lower extremities are symmetrical

---

After reviewing the case and the Grading Criteria in Appendix A, jot down your notes or preliminary answers in the spaces provided below. When you are ready to submit your answers for grading (if you are working with an instructor) and reflective feedback to help you evaluate your answers, go to **http://www.evolve.elsevier.com/Cappiello/** to complete this case.

Learning Issues

Before identifying your recommended Assessment and Plan, identify any learning issues that you believe are important for you to explore about this case:

Assessment

Please indicate the problems or issues you have identified that will guide your care (preferably in list form):

Plan

Please list your plans for addressing each of the problems or issues in your assessment:

Case 47

4:00 PM

Erin Smith

Age 25 years

Opening Scenario

Erin Smith is a 25-year-old single woman here to discuss weight loss.

History of Present Illness

"I'm here to discuss the new weight loss pills. I read about this in *Time Magazine* and discussed this with my family. We think it could work for me. I'm 5 feet 5 and ½ inches tall and weigh 195 pounds. My weight has increased 15 pounds in the past six months. I have always been somewhat overweight. Two-and-a-half years ago I tried Weight Watchers and lost 15 pounds. I'm using the diet now, but have not rejoined and gone to meetings. I work out on a treadmill a half hour most days of the week since the weather turned cold.; before that, I walked one mile each day with the dog."

Medical History

Seen here previously for two visits—six months ago for a well-woman visit including contraception prescribing, then three months later for a review of her oral contraceptives. No history of major medical illnesses. Tonsillectomy and adenoidectomy at age eight.

Family Medical History

MGM & MGF: Both died in auto accident in their 60s
PGM: MI(myocardial infarction at age 70, now doing well)
PGF: Type 2 DM in his late 60s
Father: 48 years old; A&W; height 5 ft 10 in, weight 175 lb
Mother: 48 years old; A&W; height 5 ft 6 in, weight 160 lb
Sister: 16 years old; height 5 ft 6 in, weight 135 lb

Social History

Works as a secretary and lives at home with parents, sister, and uncle. No caffeine use, alcohol use only once a month. Nonsmoker. Denies drug use. Sleeps eight hours per night. Uses seatbelt occasionally. Past history of dating violence. Currently has boyfriend for one year who is not abusive, good relationship. See History of Present Illness for exercise.

Medications

Ortho-Novum 1/35

Allergies

Sulfa drugs

Dietary History

24-hour recall
Breakfast: Orange juice (8 oz), bagel with cream cheese; muffin midmorning
Lunch: Sandwich, diet cola
Dinner: Quarter of roast chicken, potato salad about a cup, large glass of orange juice – probably 12 ounces.
Evening: Nachos with cheese, at least 12 chips.

Review of Systems

General: Feels healthy overall; denies sleeplessness, lack of appetite, lack of energy or interest in life; feels happy
Integumentary: No rashes, lesions, itching, bruising
HEENT: States vision and hearing normal; occasional head cold, no sinusitis or post-nasal drip; no history of allergies; states no problems in mouth, regular dental care
Cardiovascular: No history of heart murmur, chest pain, palpitations, dizziness, or exercise intolerance
Respiratory: No history of asthma, bronchitis, shortness of breath
Breasts: No masses, nipple discharge
Gastrointestinal: No problems with heartburn, nausea, vomiting, stomach pain, constipation, diarrhea
Genitourinary: Negative history for UTIs; G1P0; abortion one to two years ago; gynecological examination six months ago; previous two Paps WNL within normal limits and yearly chlamydia screen negative; diagnosed with bacterial vaginosis six months ago—cleared with Metro-Gel use for five days; light menses on oral

contraceptive pills; LMP two weeks ago; sexually active with boyfriend for one year, monogamous, does not use condoms

Musculoskeletal: No history of sprains, fractures, chronic muscle pain

Endocrine: No heat or cold intolerance, sweating, change in hair distribution; only occasional fatigue; no changes in appetite

Physical Examination

Vital signs: Temperature 97.8° F; pulse 70 bpm; respirations 16/min; BP 110/62 mm Hg

Height: 5 ft 5½ in; *weight:* 195 lb; *BMI:* 33; *waist circumference:* 36 in

General: Engaged, friendly, appears comfortable

Neck: No thyromegaly or lymphadenopathy noted

Heart: Regular rate and rhythm; no murmurs, rubs, or gallops

Lungs: Lungs clear to auscultation bilaterally

Musculoskeletal: 5/5 strength all extremities

After reviewing the case and the Grading Criteria in Appendix A, jot down your notes or preliminary answers in the spaces provided below. When you are ready to submit your answers for grading (if you are working with an instructor) and reflective feedback to help you evaluate your answers, go to http://www.evolve.elsevier.com/Cappiello/ to complete this case.

Learning Issues

Before identifying your recommended Assessment and Plan, identify any learning issues that you believe are important for you to explore about this case:

Assessment

Please indicate the problems or issues you have identified that will guide your care (preferably in list form):

Plan

Please list your plans for addressing each of the problems or issues in your assessment:

Case 48

Wilson Metcalf

Age 64 years

Opening Scenario

Mr. Metcalf is a 64-year-old male and is a new patient on your schedule for difficulty starting his urine stream. His wife is a patient of yours, and she recommended that he come to see you. He has not been seen by a provider in several years. Mr. Metcalf had seen a physician about five years ago who had given him a prescription for nitroglycerin and did a workup for his chest pain. The cardiac workup was "negative" per the patient, and the physician told Mr. Metcalf that he thought his pain was probably gastrointestinal in origin. You are able to access an ER record from six months ago, the results of which are noted below.

History of Present Illness

"I noticed about one year ago that my urine stream was decreasing slightly. Now I have to stand for a couple of minutes before I can urinate. I have to get up once or twice a night to urinate, disrupting my sleep." Mr. Metcalf denies hematuria and dysuria. He feels that his bladder does not empty completely. He urinates about every two or three hours during the day.

Your medical assistant (MA) gave him an International Prostate Symptoms Score (IPSS) scale and he scored 13 (0–7 = mild symptoms, 8–19 = moderate symptoms, 20–35 = severe symptoms).

Medical History

He still has his occasional "angina" (about three times a year), but it is completely relieved by rest. Has not tried antacids, H_2 blockers, or proton pump inhibitors (PPIs). He says he was told that his electrocardiogram (ECG) was completely normal, and he says he had an exercise tolerance test (ETT), which was normal (meaning without any evidence of ischemic changes). The ETT did not reproduce the pain. He had an appendectomy at age 19. He started taking diazepam (Valium) because he was feeling extremely stressed at work about 10 years ago. He has gone to urgent care a couple of times to get refills and adds, "Oh, and I really need a refill on that one, too."

Family Medical History

Maternal grandmother: Bilateral amputations from vascular disease
Mother: 85 years old (type 2 DM), lives in a local nursing home
Father: Deceased at age 79 (cerebral infarct; partial gastrectomy at 38)
Brother: 60 years old (A&W)
Three children: 27, 29, and 32 years old (A&W)

Social History

Bank loan officer. Drinks two to three beers per night. Has smoked one pack of cigarettes per day for 40 years. Married.

Medications

Valium: 5 mg in morning daily as needed
Nitroglycerin: 0.4 mg sublingually for chest pain as needed

Allergies

NKDA

Review of Systems

General: Denies night sweats, swelling
Integumentary: No excessive bruising
HEENT: Denies diplopia, blurring, hearing impairment, sore throats, chest pain, shortness of breath, dyspnea on exertion, paroxysmal nocturnal dyspnea
Gastrointestinal: Denies nausea, vomiting, constipation, diarrhea, anorexia, black or clay-colored stools
Genitourinary: Denies dysuria, hematuria
Musculoskeletal: Denies joint and back pain
Neurological: Denies fevers or chills

Physical Examination

Vital signs: Temperature 98.9° F; pulse 82 bpm; respirations 18/min; BP 122/82 mm Hg
Height: 5 ft 11 in; *weight:* 220 lb; *BMI:* 30.7
HEENT: Head is normocephalic, atraumatic; pupils equal, round, and reactive to light; extraocular movements intact; tympanic membranes are observable without excessive cerumen; nares are patent without redness or exudate; throat is noninjected; tongue is midline; palate rises symmetrically; teeth are in adequate repair

Neck: Supple; without thyromegaly, adenopathy, or carotid bruits
Heart: Regular rate and rhythm; no murmurs, rubs, or gallops
Lungs: Clear to auscultation and percussion
Abdomen: Soft, nontender; no hepatosplenomegaly
Gastrointestinal: Brown stool; no masses
Genitourinary: Prostate is firm, symmetrical, mildly enlarged (3 fingerbreadths wide); genitalia are normal, circumcised male; testicles descended bilaterally; bladder not palpable; no urge to void on suprapubic palpation
Extremities: Without cyanosis, clubbing, or edema
Neurological: Reflexes are 2+ at the biceps, triceps, brachioradialis, patellar, and Achilles; no Babinski signs present; strength and sensation are symmetrical

Laboratory Results for Wilson Metcalf from Six Months Ago

Seen in emergency room about six months ago for a suspected pneumonia, but chest x-ray examination was negative. Mr. Metcalfe was treated for bronchitis and did well. In your electronic medical record, you can see a copy of his complete blood count (CBC) (Table 48-1), chemistry profile (Table 48-2), and urinalysis (Table 48-3) from that visit. ECG is without evidence of ischemia or ectopy. He did get a prescription for diazepam at that visit.

You repeat his ECG today and it continues to be normal.

TABLE 48-1	CBC for Wilson Metcalf from 6 Months Ago	
CBC	Result	Normal Range
WBC	9.9	4.5–10.8
RBC	5.1	4.2–5.4
Hgb	14.1	12.0–16.0
Hct	40.2	37.0–47.0
MCV	92.2	87.0–99.0
MCH	28.2	27.0–32.0
MCHC	32.8	32.0–36.0
RDW	13.7	11.0–16.0
Platelets	396	150–450
Segs	55	50–65
Lymphocytes	31	25–45
Monocytes	10	0–10
Eosinocytes	4	0–4

TABLE 48-2	Chemistry Profile for Wilson Metcalf from 6 Months Ago	
Test	Result	Normal Range
FBS	103	60–110
BUN	27	8–28
Creatinine	1.1	0.5–1.5
Sodium	138	135–145
Potassium	4.3	3.5–5.5
Chloride	101	95–105
Albumin	4.8	4.0–6.0
Total protein	7.3	6.5–8.0
Alkaline phosphate	100	30–120
ALT	22	0–40
AST	20	0–40
LDH	144	50–150
Cholesterol	200	110–200
GGT	26	0–30
Magnesium	2.2	1.6–2.4
Bilirubin	0.6	0.1–1.0
Conjugated bilirubin	0.1	0.0–0.2
Iron	80	60–160
Uric acid	6.4	2.0–7.0

TABLE 48-3	Urinalysis for Wilson Metcalf from 6 Months Ago	
Test	Result	
Color	Yellow	
Character	Clear	
Specific gravity	1.015	
pH	6.0	
Glucose	Negative	
Nitrite	Negative	
Protein	Negative	
Leukocytes	Negative	
Blood	Negative	

After reviewing the case and the Grading Criteria in Appendix A, jot down your notes or preliminary answers in the spaces provided below. When you are ready to submit your answers for grading (if you are working with an instructor) and reflective feedback to help you evaluate your answers, go to **http://www.evolve.elsevier.com/Cappiello/** to complete this case.

Learning Issues

Before identifying your recommended Assessment and Plan, identify any learning issues that you believe are important for you to explore about this case:

Assessment

Please indicate the problems or issues you have identified that will guide your care (preferably in list form):

Plan

Please list your plans for addressing each of the problems or issues in your assessment:

Case 49

4:45 PM

Kimberly Parsons
Age 16 years

Part 1

Opening Scenario

Kimberly Parsons is a 16-year-old female adolescent who is in your office for a 15-minute visit. Her mother is not present because she works and could not take the day off, but she did provide written consent for diagnosis and treatment. Ms. Parsons says that her mother said to call her if there were any problems or questions. Kimberly has been coming to this practice for several years, but this is the first time you have seen her.

History of Present Illness

"I go through periods when I cough a lot. I never cough up anything; it's just a dry, hacking cough. I have coughing episodes after I swim in the pool, and it seems like I just can't take a deep breath. I don't think I had this before last summer. It is actually better since I've been swimming in the pool, but I still cough when I get out. It was really bad last summer when I was at my grandmother's camp. I've never felt like I was wheezing." Ms. Parsons has four to five colds per year.

Medical History

Never hospitalized, no major accidents, no chronic illnesses. Her medical record shows previous visits for well-child checks; three episodes of otitis media, all before age 18 months; and four upper respiratory infections (URIs) that she came to the office for between ages two and 10. No surgeries.

Family Medical History

MGM, MGF, PGM, PGF –A&W, no known health problems
Father: 45 years old, A&W
Mother: 45 years old, A&W

Social History

Does not smoke or drink alcohol. Lives with parents. She is an "A" student.

Medications

Occasional Dimetapp and Advil

Allergies

NKDA

Review of Systems

General: Denies weight change, sleep problems; feeling well except for cough
Integumentary: Denies rashes or lesions; had eczema as a baby
HEENT: Denies frequent sore throats, headaches, ear pain, blurred or double vision
Cardiovascular: Denies chest pain, shortness of breath; good exercise tolerance, except as noted above; no bruising
Hematological: No bruising
Respiratory: Hacking cough, nonproductive; denies shortness of breath, good exercise tolerance
Gastrointestinal: Occasional diarrhea with high stress; denies nausea, vomiting, indigestion; gets gassy when she drinks milk
Genitourinary: No itching or discharge; never had sexually transmitted disease (STD) testing; LMP 2 weeks ago, 5 days normal flow; no dysmenorrhea; denies current or previous sexual activity; no dysuria

Physical Examination

Vital signs: Temperature 98.4° F; pulse 70 bpm; respirations 24/min; BP 110/60 mm Hg
Height: 5 ft 5 in; *weight:* 120 lb; *BMI:* 20.0
General: Appears stated age, well groomed; cooperative; oriented to time and place
HEENT: Head is normocephalic, atraumatic; pupils equal, round, and reactive to light; extraocular movements intact; tympanic membranes observable without excessive cerumen; nares are patent without redness or exudate; nasal mucosa is a little pale; throat is noninjected; tongue is midline; palate rises symmetrically; teeth are in adequate repair
Neck: Supple without thyromegaly or adenopathy
Heart: Regular rate and rhythm; no murmurs, rubs, or gallops
Lungs: Clear to auscultation and percussion; peak expiratory flow rates (PEFRs): 290/310/320; her predicted is 453
Abdominal: Soft, nontender; no hepatosplenomegaly

Part 2

"While I'm here, I was wondering if you could give me some birth control pills. I'm not having sex yet, but I think I'm going to soon." How will you respond to her request?

After reviewing the case and the Grading Criteria in Appendix A, jot down your notes or preliminary answers in the spaces provided below. When you are ready to submit your answers for grading (if you are working with an instructor) and reflective feedback to help you evaluate your answers, go to **http://www.evolve.elsevier.com/ Cappiello/** to complete this case.

Learning Issues

Before identifying your recommended Assessment and Plan, identify any learning issues that you believe are important for you to explore about this case:

Assessment

Please indicate the problems or issues you have identified that will guide your care (preferably in list form):

Plan

Please list your plans for addressing each of the problems or issues in your assessment:

Case 50

Staff Meeting to Review Financials

Opening Scenario

You received the following e-mail:

> *"Just a reminder of the staff meeting that will be held at the end of business today. We will primarily be discussing the need for providers to improve their RVUs (relative value units) (specifically work RVUs) and overall reimbursement. Less than 50% of the providers made meaningful use last year and we will also need to improve this rate as well. Please bring any ideas that you have for improving these numbers."*

You also receive a second e-mail:

> *"Hi, just wanted you to have your RVUs (work) from the past three months in preparation for tonight's meeting:*
> *Month 1: 216 (you worked 18 days that months and generated 12 RVUs per day)*
> *Month 2: 231*
> *Month 3: 182 (you were off a week that month)"*

You have to get ready for this meeting. What do you need to know about the business side of things? You may not have enough time to figure everything out before tonight, but what kinds of things will you need to learn quickly to survive financially in this environment?

After reviewing the case and the Grading Criteria in Appendix A, jot down your notes or preliminary answers in the spaces provided below. When you are ready to submit your answers for grading (if you are working with an instructor) and reflective feedback to help you evaluate your answers, go to **http://www.evolve.elsevier.com/Cappiello/** to complete this case.

Learning Issues

Before identifying your recommended Assessment and Plan, identify any learning issues that you believe are important for you to explore about this case:

Assessment

Please indicate the problems or issues you have identified that will guide your your planning for this meeting (preferably in list form):

Plan

Please list your plans for addressing each of the problems or issues in your assessment:

Appendix A

Grading Criteria: Assessment and Plan Write-Up (generic)

	Exceeds	Meets	Needs Improvement	Unacceptable
Assessment	Assessment is based on documentation provided. Clear justification for diagnoses. Includes all secondary problems. Highly cost effective when ordering diagnostic tests and therapeutic options. Elicits patient perspective.	Assessment is based on documentation provided. Clear justification for diagnoses. Includes all primary and some secondary problems. Cost effective when ordering diagnostic tests and therapeutic options.	Assessment is partially based on documentation provided. Incomplete justification for diagnoses. Includes some of the primary and/or secondary problems. No awareness of cost effectiveness when ordering diagnostic tests and therapeutic options.	Assessment is not consistent with documentation provided. Fails to clearly justify primary diagnosis or note secondary problems. Inappropriate or incomplete diagnostic plan.
Plan—pharmacologic	Treatment plan reflects individualized application of evidence-based data. Choices are highly cost effective. Interactions with other medications, OTCs, and diet are considered.	Treatment plan reflects evidence-based data. Choices are cost effective. Interactions with other medications and OTCs are considered.	Treatment plan reflects some use of evidence-based data. Choices are not cost aware but are appropriate. Interactions with other medications are considered.	Treatment plan reflects individualized application of evidence-based data. Choices are highly cost effective. Interactions with other medications, OTCs, and diet are considered.
Plan— nonpharmacologic	Identifies areas for additional data collection. Treatment recommendations and patient education address all issues raised by diagnoses and are individualized, evidence-based interventions. Highly cost effective treatment.	Treatment recommendations and patient education address all primary and some secondary issues that are raised by diagnoses and are evidence-based interventions. Cost effective treatment.	Some treatment recommendations and patient education address primary and/or secondary issues but are not evidence-based interventions and/or cost effective.	Minimal nonpharmacologic treatment plan and/or patient education are not addressed.
Follow-up	Timing and type of follow-up is thoughtfully addressed.	Follow-up is adequately addressed.	Follow-up is addressed, but timing or type of follow-up is suboptimal.	No follow-up is indicated.
Organization and format	All information is organized in a logical sequence and follows an acceptable format.	Information is generally organized in a logical sequence and follows acceptable format.	Minor errors in format; information is suboptimally organized.	Major errors in format; information is disorganized.

Appendix B

Abbreviations

3 fb↑sp	Three finger-breadths above the symphysis pubis	**AHRQ**	Agency for Healthcare Policy and Research	**BPH**	Benign prostatic hyperplasia
@umb	At umbilicus	**ALT**	Alanine transaminase	**BRB**	Bright-red blood
A&W	Alive and well			**BUN**	Blood urea nitrogen
AA	Alcoholics Anonymous	**AIDS**	Acquired immunodeficiency syndrome	**CAD**	Coronary artery disease
AACE	American Association of Clinical Endocrinologists	**ASA**	Acetylsalicylic acid (aspirin)	**CAGE**	Cut down, Annoyed, Guilty, Eye-opener
ACS	American Cancer Society	**ASCUS**	Atypical cells of undetermined significance	**CARE**	Cholesterol and Recurrent Events
ACC	American College of Cardiology	**ASCVD**	Arteriosclerotic cardiovascular disease	**CBC**	Complete blood count
ACD	Anemia of chronic disease	**AST**	Aspartate aminotransferase	**CCAIT**	Canadian Atherosclerosis Intervention Trial
ACEI	Angiotensin-converting enzyme inhibitor	**ATRIA**	Anticoagulation and Risk Factors in Atrial Fibrillation	**CDC**	Centers for Disease Control and Prevention
ACOG	American Congress of Obstetricians and Gynecologists and American College of Obstetricians and Gynecologists	**AUA**	American Urological Association	**CF**	Cystic fibrosis
				CFS	Chronic fatigue syndrome
		AUDIT	Alcohol Use Disorders Identification Test	**CG-CAHPS**	Clinician and Groups–Consumer Assessment of Healthcare Providers and Systems
ACP	American College of Physicians	**AV/AF**	Anteverted/anteflexed	**CHADS**	Congestive heart failure, hypertension, age, diabetes mellitus, prior stroke or TIA or thromboembolism
ADA	American Diabetes Association	**AWV**	Annual wellness visit		
ADLs	Activities of daily living	**BCG**	Bacillus Calmette-Guérin		
AED	Automated external defibrillator	**bid**	Twice a day	**CHADS-VASC**	same as CHADS with vascular, advanced age, and sex category added
		BM	Bowel movement		
AFP	Alpha-fetoprotein	**BMI**	Body mass index		
AHA	American Heart Association	**BNP**	B-type natriuretic peptide		
		BP	Blood pressure		

CHD	Coronary heart disease	**EHR/EMR**	Electronic health record/electronic medical record
CHF	Congestive heart failure	**EMTALA**	Emergency Medical Treatment and Labor Act
CK	Creatinine kinase		
CLIA	Clinical Laboratory Improvement Act	**ENT**	Ears, nose, and throat
CMS	Centers for Medicare and Medicaid Services	**ER**	Emergency room
		ESR	Erythrocyte sedimentation rate
CNM	Certified nurse midwife	**ETOH**	Alcohol
CMT	Cervical motion tenderness	**ETT**	Exercise tolerance test
COPD	Chronic obstructive pulmonary disease	**FABERE**	Flexion, abduction, external rotation, and extension
CPT	Current Procedural Terminology	**FBS**	Fasting blood sugar
CT	Computed tomography	**FDA**	Food and Drug Administration
CVA	Costovertebral angle; cerebrovascular accident	**FPG**	Fasting plasma glucose
		FHR	Fetal heart rate
CXR	Chest x-ray	**FIT**	Fecal immunochemical test
DEXA	Dual-energy x-ray absorptiometry	**FOBT**	Fecal occult blood test
DJD	Degenerative joint disease	**GABHS**	Group A beta-hemolytic streptococci
DMPA	Depomedroxyprogesterone acetate		
DM	Diabetes mellitus	**GC**	Gonorrhea
DP	Dorsalis pedis pulse	**GCPS**	Guide to Clinical Preventive Services
DPT	Diphtheria-pertussis-tetanus	**GDS**	Geriatric Depression Scale
DPOA	Durable power of attorney	**GERD**	Gastroesophageal reflux disease
DRE	Digital rectal examination	**GFR**	Glomerular filtration rate
DS	Double strength	**GGT**	Gamma-glutamyl transferase
DTaP	Diphtheria, tetanus, a cellular pertussis	**GTT**	Glucose tolerance test
TdaP	Tetanus, diphtheria, acellular pertussis	**GxPx**	Gravida = number of pregnancies Para = outcome of each pregnancy Para includes (in this order) number of term pregnan-
ECG	Electrocardiogram		
ECP	Emergency contraceptive pill		
EDC	Estimated date of confinement		
EF	Ejection fraction		

cies, preterm pregnancies, number of abortions (spontaneous or induced), ectopic pregnancies, and number of living children.

HASBLED	Hypertension (uncontrolled, >160 mm Hg systolic), abnormal renal/liver function, stroke, bleeding history or predisposition (anemia), labile INR (i.e., therapeutic time in range <60%), elderly (>65), and drugs/alcohol concomitantly (antiplatelet agents, nonsteroidal antiinflammatory drugs) (maximum score 9)
HBV	Hepatitis B virus
HAV	Hepatitis A virus
HCl	Hydrochloric acid
HCM	Hypertrophic cardiomyopathy
Hct	Hematocrit
HDL	High-density lipoprotein
HEENT	Head, eyes, ears, nose, throat
HELLP	Hypertension, elevated liver function, low platelets syndrome
Hgb	Hemoglobin
HGSIL	High-grade squamous intraepithelial lesion
Hib	*Haemophilus influenzae* type b
HIV	Human immunodeficiency virus
HMO	Health maintenance organization
HNP	Herniated nucleus pulposus

HPI	History of present illness	**LDL**	Low-density lipoprotein	**NCEP**	National Cholesterol Education Program
HPV	Human papillomavirus	**LE**	Lower extremity	**NICE**	National Institute for Health and Care Excellence (UK)
HRT	Hormone replacement therapy	**LFT**	Liver function test		
		LGSIL	Low-grade squamous intraepithelial lesion	**NIPT**	Non-Invasive Prenatal Testing
HSV	Herpes simplex virus	**LMP**	Last menstrual period	**NNT**	Number needed to treat
HTN	Hypertension	**LNG-IUD**	Levonorgestrel intrauterine device	**NSAID**	Nonsteroidal antiinflammatory drug
IADLs	Instrumental activities of daily living				
IBD	Inflammatory bowel disease	**LRI**	Lower respiratory infection	**NSVD**	Normal spontaneous vaginal delivery
IBS	Irritable bowel syndrome	**LSB**	Left sternal border		
		MA	Medical assistant	**OAB**	Overactive bladder
IBW	Ideal body weight	**MAO**	Monoamine oxidase	**OC/OCP**	Oral contraceptive/oral contraceptive pill
ICS	Intercostal space				
ID	Intradermal	**MAST**	Michigan Alcoholism Screening Test		
IDA	Iron-deficiency anemia			**OGTT**	Oral glucose tolerance test
IDDM	Insulin-dependent diabetes mellitus	**MCH**	Mean corpuscular hemoglobin	**OPV**	Oral poliovirus vaccine
IDSA	Infectious Diseases Society of America	**M-CHAT**	Modified Checklist for Autism in Toddlers	**OSA**	Obstructive sleep apnea
IGRA	Interferon-gamma release assay	**MCHC**	Mean corpuscular hemoglobin concentration	**OTC**	Over the counter
				PCMH	Patient-centered medical home
IHSS	Idiopathic hypertrophic subaortic stenosis	**MCL**	Midclavicular line		
		MCV	Mean corpuscular volume	**PCP**	*Pneumocystis carinii* pneumonia
INH	Isonicotinic acid hydrazide	**MDI**	Metered dose inhaler	**PCR**	Polymerase chain reaction
INR	International normalized ratio	**MGF**	Maternal grandfather	**PCV13**	Pneumococcal conjugate vaccine
IPPE	Initial Preventive Physical Examination (Medicare)	**MGM**	Maternal grandmother	**PEFR**	Peak expiratory flow rate
		MI	Myocardial infarction	**PFT**	Pulmonary function test
IPSS	International Prostate Symptom Score	**mm Hg**	Millimeters of mercury	**PGF**	Paternal grandfather
IPV	Inactivated poliovirus vaccine	**MMR**	Measles-mumps-rubella	**PGM**	Paternal grandmother
IUD	Intrauterine device	**MMSE**	Mini Mental Status Examination	**PID**	Pelvic inflammatory disease
IV	Intravenous				
JVD	Jugular venous distention	**MPV**	Mean platelet volume	**PIH**	Pregnancy-induced hypertension
LBP	Low back pain	**MRI**	Magnetic resonance imaging	**PMI**	Point of maximal impulse
LDCT	Low-dose computed tomography				
LDH	Lactic dehydrogenase	**MVP**	Mitral valve prolapse	**PMS**	Premenstrual syndrome

PND	Paroxysmal nocturnal dyspnea; postnasal drip	**Segs**	Segmented neutrophils	**TCN**	Tetracycline
PO	Per os (by mouth)	**SG**	Specific gravity	**Td**	Tetanus-diphtheria
PPI	Proton pump inhibitor	**SGOT**	Serum glutamic oxaloacetic transaminase (also known as AST)	**Tdap**	Tetanus, diphtheria, acellular pertussis (lowercase letters indicate lower concentrations)
PPD	Purified protein derivative				
PPSV23	Pneumococcal polysaccharide vaccine	**SHEP**	Systolic Hypertension in the Elderly Project	**TIA**	Transient ischemic attack
pr	Per rectum	**SI**	Sacroiliac	**TIBC**	Total iron-binding capacity
prn	As needed	**SIADH**	Syndrome of inappropriate antidiuretic hormone	**tid**	Three times a day
PSA	Prostate-specific antigen			**TMJ**	Temporomandibular joint
PSO	Predicted serum osmolality	**SL**	Sublingual	**TMP/SMX**	Trimethoprim/sulfamethoxazole
PT	Posterior tibial pulse; physical therapy	**SLIT**	Sublingual immunotherapy	**TSH**	Thyroid-stimulating hormone
		SLR	Straight-leg raise	**TUG**	Timed Up and Go test
PVR	Postvoid residual	**SNAP**	Safety Net Antibiotic Prescription	**TZD**	Thiazolidinedione
qd	Every day			**UI**	Urinary incontinence
qid	Four times a day	**SOB**	Shortness of breath		
qxh	Every (#) hours			**URI**	Upper respiratory infection
RBC	Red blood cell	**s/p**	Status post		
RDA	Recommended Daily Allowance	**SPECT**	Single-photon emission computed tomography	**US**	Ultrasound
				USPSTF	U.S. Preventive Services Task Force
RDW	Red cell distribution width	**SSRI**	Selective serotonin reuptake inhibitor		
RHF	Rheumatic heart fever	**STD**	Sexually transmitted disease	**UTI**	Urinary tract infection
RPR	Rapid plasma reagin	**STI**	Sexually transmitted infection	**UV**	Ultraviolet
				VZIG	Varicella-zoster immune globulin
RVUs	Relative value units				
4S	Scandinavian Simvastatin Survival Study	**SU**	Sulfonylurea	**VZV**	Varicella-zoster virus
		T2DM	Type 2 diabetes mellitus (do not use Roman numerals)		
SC	Subcutaneously			**WBC**	White blood cell
SCIT	Subcutaneous immunotherapy	**T&A**	Tonsillectomy and adenoidectomy	**WCC**	Well-child check
				WHO	World Health Organization
SCOR	Specialized Center of Research	**TAB**	Therapeutic abortion	**WOSCOPS**	West of Scotland Coronary Prevention Study
SD	Standard deviation	**TB**	Tuberculosis		
SEER	Surveillance, Epidemiology, and End Results	**TCA**	Tricyclic antidepressant	**wRVUs**	Work Relative Value Units

Index

Page numbers followed by *f* indicate figures, *t* indicate tables and *b* indicate boxes.